Epee 2.0
The Birth of the New Fencing Paradigm

Epee 2.0
The Birth of the New Fencing Paradigm

Johan Harmenberg

With Ruggero Ceci, Geoff Pingree, and Björne Väggö

SKA SwordPlay Books

Photographic Credits

Cover and p. 17 [JH vs. Riboud] by Lars Nyberg,
　1980. Courtesy of *Expressen*, Stockholm.
30.　[MIT Fencing Team with "Little Iron Man,"] 1974.
　The Tech, MIT.
97.　[JH vs. Popa], by Gunnar Lundmark, 1980.
　Courtesy of SCP-Fotopool, Scandia Photopress.
97.　[Three Swedish Gold Medalists],, 1980.
　Courtesy of photographer Hans Gedda..
98.　[JH with Olympic Gold], by Lars Nyberg, 1980.
　Courtesy of *Expressen*, Stockholm.
138.[Björne on the podium], 1984.
　Courtesy of photographer Thore Leykauff.
Other photographs courtesy of their subjects.

Published by SKA SwordPlay Books
SKA SwordPLay Books
3939 Victory Boulevard
Staten Island, NY 10314
Web: www.swordplaybooks.com
E-mail: publisher@swordplaybooks.com

Printed in the United States of America

Table of Contents

Figures and Tables

Dedication

This book is dedicated to Eric Sollee, whose Three Conjectures and detailed questioning of me in 1973 led both to my subsequent fencing success and to the thought processes that resulted in this book.

Acknowledgements

I have been privileged to enjoy the guidance, partnership and personal exchange of ideas with no less than four outstanding coaches: Rudolf Meckel, Eric Sollee, Kaj Czarnecki and Salek Altauz. The contributions of the three former have been covered in the book but Salek Altauz should be acknowledged for adding the final touches before the 1980 Olympics.

Of utmost importance for the compilation of this book has been my collaboration with my co-writers Björne Väggö, Geoff Pingree and Ruggero Ceci. Björne has not only been instrumental as a discussion partner over the years, he is also a very good friend and should be acknowledged for bearing with me as a room mate in all of those boring training camps.

Also instrumental for this book has been my publisher/editor/collaborator Steve Khinoy. He has asked all of the critical questions and he has surprisingly rapidly understood the inner concepts of the new paradigm. I sometimes feel that he understands the consequences of the paradigm better than I. Thanks also to Malcolm Fare for his painstaking editorial work.

I also want to thank the juniors in Sweden who willingly let me change their fencing styles around and had to bear with me when I tested out different ways to teach the paradigm. I have also appreciated my discussions with Johan Bergdahl.

I naturally want to thank all of my fencing friends on both sides of the Atlantic, especially the three clubs that I have regarded from time to time as mine. These include Bygdö Fäktklubb (Oslo, Norway) and MIT fencing (Cambridge, Massachusetts, USA) but especially the fencing club in Stockholm where I have been fencing for more than 40 years; Föreningen för Fäktkonstens Främjande (roughly, "The Association for the Advancement of the Art of Fencing") also called FFF. I have also appreciated the more recent collaboration with Harvard fencing (Cambridge, Mass. USA).

Last but not least, I would like to thank my family – especially my lovely wife, Ulrika.

A Caution and an Invitation

When writing a book about fencing strategy, the concepts are based directly or indirectly on ideas passed through generations. I have already acknowledged the contributions of my coaches. In addition, many of the ideas have been borrowed from a variety of sources, not all of which have been highlighted in the text. My ideas, in other words, are not all new. I believe, however, that the compilation of these ideas into a paradigm is connected with a certain amount of novelty.

Furthermore, in order to present the concepts as clearly as possible, I have found it necessary to make this book a bit too binary (black or white) for my own taste. The world is not black and white and this is especially valid for fencing strategy. As a scientist, I disapprove of this compromise, but including all the qualifications, all the ifs and buts, would lengthen the book unbearably without making it any clearer. If I have thereby unintentionally offended any reader, I would like to comfort that reader with the thought that the ifs and buts can be included in later publications by others or me.

I have tried to be as honest as possible in setting out my own views, and I readily acknowledge that other thinkers may have theirs. I would welcome discussion. I see the present book as just a first step in describing the present fencing paradigm of fencing strategy from my own experience, and I sincerely hope that the paradigm will continue to develop over time with contributions from others.

Terminology

It is not within the scope of this book to provide a complete glossary of fencing terms.

However, terminology varies from country to country and even within a country's borders. The names and descriptions of the hand positions, in particular, vary widely, and we have provided descriptions of them in section A.1.

In addition, the terms used here for several familiar actions may not be familiar to all. Some of these are given in section 1.2.

Tournament formats during the period covered by this book were undergoing steady change; the differences between then and now are set out in section 1.3.

Finally, the New Fencing Paradigm which is this book's main subject has required the creation of a new vocabulary. Accordingly, the reader would be well advised to review section 4, which also includes some abbreviations and terms which may not be familiar to non-US readers.

A. Fencing Actions

A.1 *The positions and parries*
We will limit ourselves to those actually used in this book.

Notes:
1) "Pronated" means "with the palm / nails facing downward;" "supinated" means "with the palm / nails facing upward." In what follows, where the word "pronated" or "supinated" is used, "semi-pronated" or "semi-supinated" could be substituted.

2) Hand positions are approximate, not absolute.

After some hesitation, we have decided to adopt the modern English "first, second, third, fourth, etc." rather than the traditional "prime, seconde, tierce, quarte, etc." The reason is that the modern terms should be comprehensible even to readers who are familiar with the traditional ones, while the reverse may not be the case. Hence:

SECOND (seconde): the low outside pronated position and parry, the thumb horizontal and the palm facing downward.

FOURTH (quarte): the high inside position and parry that is not fully pronated. Full pronation would be fifth (quinte.) I myself execute this parry with my hand toward pronation (thumb about 10 o'clock).

SIXTH (sixte): the high outside supinated position and parry, with thumb at approximately one o'clock for a right-handed fencer.

SEVENTH (septime) the low inside supinated position and parry, with the thumb pointing downward and inward.

EIGHTH (octave), the low outside supinated position and parry, with the thumb pointing downward and outward.

A.2 Actions and general vocabulary

BIND: The term "bind" throughout this book is used in a different sense from that of the French School *liement*. As used here, a bind is a thrust that maintains contact with the opponent's blade and uses the position of the hand and guard to deflect the opponent's point and blade from the target. Put another way, binds are thrusts with opposition. Binds can be attacks, counterattacks, or ripostes. It is important to note that throughout this book, it is stressed that there is little difference between offensive and defensive blade actions.

BLOCKING: Action of the arm and guard that prevents the opponent from touching while making only incidental use of blade-to-blade contact. If one fencer defends himself by deflecting the incoming point and blade with his guard without using the blade, we call this "blocking of the scoring attempt." If the two fencers end up with locked guards, one or both of the fencers may elect to avoid the opponents scoring attempt through preserving the guard lock. This case we also call "blocking." Blocking sometimes look like that moment in a movie swordfight when the opponents lock guards and glare at each other. A third possibility is shown in the cover photo, where the opponent is trying, unsuccessfully, to block my scoring attempt by locking my weapon arm with his guard.

BOUNCE: A jump forward, backward, or in place, that lands on the toes of both feet simultaneously. To bounce is to execute a series of these jumps.

COMPULSIVE PUSH-BACKERS: Fencers who always push back against pressure on their blade.

FRENCH HANDLER: Fencer who fences with a French grip, often held at the pommel. Also known as pommelers.

PISTE (Strip): The internationally accepted term for what is called in the US the fencing strip.

POMMELER: See French Handler.

POOL (Poule): The internationally accepted word is the French poule, which means a chicken (don't ask!), but the US spelling is "pool."

STOP HIT (arrest, *arrêt*, time thrust, *coup de temps*): Used in this book to mean a counterattack, whether designed to score by hitting first or by touching with opposition.

A.3 Tournament formats

Today, most international individual competitions employ a round of 5-touch pools which is used to seed the competitors into a direct elimination (DE) format (a bracket system of 15-touch bouts where the loser is eliminated).

The Olympic Games use DE from the start, seeded by the results of previous competitions. A team competition is conducted by direct elimination.

Team matches are conducted by the relay system to a total of 45 touches.

In the period when this story begins, tournaments were conducted by a system of pools throughout, leading to a final pool of six. Because of widespread cheating (discussed in this book), this was replaced by a mixed system in which pools were followed by DE rounds of 10-touch bouts with repechage (a losers' bracket) to create a final pool of six. This was the system in use until the 1980 Olympic Games. By the 1984 Olympics, the system had changed again, preliminary pools followed by DE's of 10-touch bouts all the way to a two-man final. In the end, this led to the present system, which calls for 15-touch DE's.

Throughout the period of this book, a team match consisted of two four-man teams fencing 5-touch bouts.

B. Special vocabulary and abbreviations

Briefly put, the new paradigm calls for a fencer to develop an *area of excellence (AoE)*, to avoid the opponent's (OP's) area of excellence by taking away the conditions (his *hidden prerequisites)* that OP requires to execute his favored actions and by *steering* OP into his own AoE by controlling the distance and by the use of *confusing* or *destructive* parries. A fuller glossary follows.

AoE: *See* Area of Excellence

AFLA: The Amateur Fencers League of America, the name of the US national fencing organization before it changed to the US Fencing Association. *See* USFA.

AREA OF EXCELLENCE (AoE): A fencer's favorite and most effective moves as formulated by the new strategy.

ARM SPEED: See Point Hit Speed.

ARM – FOOT CONNECTION: The way most classical fencers learn to extend the weapon arm during offensive actions. The weapon arm is extended during the advance in order to be fully extended when the launch begins. The extension starts when the advance is started and is fully extended when the advance is complete. The unwanted consequence is that a fast advance often results in a fast weapon arm extension and a slow advance in a slow weapon arm extension, thus an arm – foot connection.

CONFUSING PARRIES: Moves that have features in common with constructive (classical) parries, but are executed with the sole intention of confusing the opponent.

CONJECTURES: The three hypotheses formulated under the guidance of MIT Coach Eric Sollee in 1973 and proved over the following decade.

CONSTRUCTIVE PARRIES: Parries executed to deflect the incoming blade; also called classical parries.

CRITICAL GAP FOR SCORING: The last 10 – 15 centimeters (4 – 6 inches) a point must cross in order to hit the target.

DE: Direct Elimination

DESTRUCTIVE PARRIES: Blade movements that have features in common with constructive parries, but are executed with the sole intention of hindering the opponent's actions. These blade movements may also be used to steer your opponent's actions into an area of your own choosing.

ECAC: The Eastern Collegiate Athletic Conference. *See* IFA.

FACILITATING HIDDEN PREREQUISITES: *See* HP's

FDC: *See* Final Decision to Commit

FIE: The Fédération Internationale d'Escrime, or International Fencing Federation, the international body governing the Olympic sport of fencing. The FIE codifies the rules and procedures which govern the sport.

FIXED BACK FOOT: A position such that the fencer's retreat is difficult or impossible because his back foot is planted.

FINAL DECISION TO COMMIT (FDC): The final, *irreversible* decision to commit to scoring in a fencing action.

FOOT SPEED: *See* Point Hit Speed.

HIDDEN PREREQUISITES (HP's): The prerequisites that a fencer needs from his opponent in order to execute his AoE. These consist of:

> *PRINCIPAL HP's:* Those prerequisites that constitute the minimum requirement for execution of a fencer's AoE, and
>
> *FACILITATING HP's:* Conditions that are helpful for the successful execution of a fencer's AoE, in addition to the principal hidden prerequisites. These facilitating HP's do not by themselves allow the execution of the AoE.

HP, HP's: *See* Hidden Prerequisites.

IFA: The Intercollegiate Fencing Association, the oldest intercollegiate fencing organization in the US. Now part of the multi-sport Eastern Collegiate Athletic Conference (ECAC), the IFA's annual tournament offers US fencing's oldest intercollegiate trophy, the Little Iron Man.

JH: Johan Harmenberg, in some photo captions and figures.

MIT: Massachusetts Institute of Technology.

NCAA: The National Collegiate Athletic Association, the most prominent and powerful governing body for intercollegiate sport in the US.

New fencing dimension: The dimension that is a sliding scale between technique-based classical tactics and physically-based new strategy tactics.

Olympic touches: Those hits that both fencers are equally *desperate* to score.

OP: The opponent.

Paradigm: Conceptual framework or overall approach.

Parries: *See Constructive Parries, Destructive Parries, Confusing Parries.* For the names and positions of the parries, see the previous section.

Point hit speed: The speed of the point of the blade when it is moving the last 10 – 15 centimeters (4 – 6 inches) towards its target to score (*See* Critical Gap for Scoring). The point speed is divided into the component caused by arm extension (arm speed) and the component caused by the foot movements (foot speed). When the point speed is related to the movement of the target, it is called relative point speed.

Quadrant: One of the four target areas or lines – high inside and outside, low inside and outside.

Relative point hit speed: *See* Point Hit Speed.

Steering actions: Actions whose only purpose is to steer an opponent's moves into an area of your own choosing.

Strategy: That part of the paradigm that is specific to an individual fencer but independent of his opponent.

Tactics: That part of the strategy that a fencer applies when facing a specific opponent.

USFA: The US Fencing Association, the national governing body of US Fencing under the Amateur Sports Act of 1978. Founded in 1898 as the Amateur Fencers League of America, its name was changed to its present form in 1981.

Frontispiece
The New Paradigm in action – Johan Harmenberg, facing us, has closed the distance and is about to score despite Riboud's attempt to block Harmenberg's arm with his guard.

Publisher's Foreword

This book tells a story. It is also a manual of instruction.

As a story, it's an inspirational tale of improbable successes against heavy odds:

- A young man abandons his fencing career. He seems to lack the talent to make it to the top. But a few years later, through steely determination and a revolutionary approach to the sport, he becomes a World Champion and Olympic gold medalist.
- An American college fencing team has languished for years in fencing obscurity. Applying this new approach, it reaches the heights of American fencing success.
- A boy is imprisoned in a World War II Japanese internment camp in the Philippines. He never sets eyes on fencing until his US Army stint in Korea. This is the coach who develops the system which brings these fencers to their improbable success.
- The new system overturns centuries of classical fencing theory and brings fencing back toward its roots as a combat art.
- In short, this book tells how epee fencing was transformed from its classical basis to a new paradigm.

As a manual of instruction, this book

- Explains the new paradigm
- Shows you its basis in theory
- Explains how it works in practice
- Gives you the means of adopting it
- Or (if you don't choose to adopt it), at least you will understand how opponents may be thinking and fencing.

The classical fencing paradigm imagines fencing as an art and as a dialogue.

As an art, fencing is conceived of as a series of positions and actions that combine elegance, grace, and power. Each action is like a statement in a debate – an assertion that calls forth an appropriate reply. Classical fencing theory uses the vocabulary of debate or drama. We speak of the phrase (*phrase d'armes*), of the conversation of the blades. The very word "riposte" (a reply, a retort) reflects this idea of a conversation.

The object of the classical fencer as artist was to weave his arguments and his opponent's answers into an elegant drama like a poem. Think of Edmond Rostand's Cyrano de Bergerac, where Cyrano composes an elaborate ballade, while dueling, ending each stanza – and eventually the duel itself – with the triumphant verse: "Then, as I end the refrain – thrust home!" The classical fencer asks himself, "How can I hit my opponent, and how can I do so with style and elegance?" The classical view was well expressed in works such as those of Egerton Castle around the beginning of the twentieth century. For Castle, fencing had *progressed* through history from simple forms to complex ones.

Another feature of the classical paradigm was the exaltation of the fencing master. As co-author Geoff Pingree writes,

> The standard model for a Fencing Master was one that had developed over hundreds of years, a model that seemed at times to be written in Hollywood. He was the holder of unique and secret knowledge, whose rituals was to be parceled out little by little to the student. The fencer's role was to be the monkish acolyte to the fencing Master's Obi-Wan Kenobi. This sense of the teacher student relationship was reinforced over the years by hundreds of fencing manuals detailing thousands of possible combinations. The fencer was to became a kind of alchemist, finding delight in the mastering of all the arcana of his sport.

While it is true that the use of a weapon, the target areas, the rules and the unique playing area of the fencing strip all required a strong training regimen for the student to understand fencing's unique physicality, this model had also inhibited the development of the modern game.

A true fencing master – in the classical sense – would rather have his students lose their bouts than fence inelegantly.

In time, the classical paradigm began to be tempered by the realities of sport fencing. Style points dropped out of favor. The Olympic Games and World Championships put an emphasis on actually winning. Electric scoring registered touches that would never have been recognized by classical fencers judging visually. By the middle of the century, works with titles like *Modern Fencing* had begun to appear.

The new paradigm builds on the actions of the old one. The actions of classical fencing remain as valid as ever. A fencer needs to master the vocabulary of classical fencing before embarking on the new system.

But the new paradigm seeks to simplify the lengthy dialogue of classical fencing. It seeks to forestall the "conversation." Rather than scheming to win a back-and-forth chess game that ends in a touch, the fencer seeks to make it as difficult as possible for his opponent to hit at all. He steers the action so as to force the opponent to attack him where he is strongest – his area of excellence. Rather than deploying a wide range of actions, he attempts to limit his actions to those few that he has rehearsed to the point of near-perfection and to carry them out with athleticism and fighting spirit.

And rather than glorifying the fencing master as the source of truth, the coach in the new paradigm is a partner in a dialogue designed to bring out the individual traits of the fencer.

In that spirit of dialogue, this book has not been written by one person only: it contains contributions by several fencers: notably Geoff Pingree, Björne Väggö, and Ruggero Ceci, as well as the principal author, Johan Harmenberg. All of them have achieved success as fencers; all have achieved distinction in their later careers.

Johan Harmenberg and Björne Väggö tell us most of their own fencing stories later in this book. Geoff Pingree contributed the material on MIT fencing, and Ruggero Ceci collaborated with Johan on the article that appears in the Appendix. Each of these collaborators adds a distinctive element.

Let's find out a little more about them.

Our Authors Today
Above, Johan Harmenberg; Below, Björne Väggö

Meet the Authors

Johan Harmenberg

Born in Stockholm in 1954, Johan took up fencing at the age of 11. As a freshman, he led the MIT foil team to the Little Iron Man trophy and a 3rd place finish in the NCAA tournament, as well as an individual 3rd place finish. He won the World Championship in individual men's epee in 1977 (the Swedish team also took first place). In 1980, he won Olympic gold in individual men's epee and finished first overall in combined World Cup results. After this, he retired from the elite international scene. In 1982, he received his doctorate in Medical Science from the Karolinska Institut in Stockholm and began a career as a physician specializing in antiviral and cancer research. He has over 100 publications and abstracts and has conducted research at firms such as Roche, AstraZeneca, Upjohn, and Medivir. Today he is CEO of Axelar AB, a cancer research company . In addition, he is on the management team for Swedish fencing, involved in training, team selection, tournament cadre, and as special advisors for junior fencers with exceptional talent. He lives in Stockholm with his wife, Ulrika. They have two children.

Björne Väggö

Björne was born in Malmö, Sweden in 1955 but lived in Göteborg (Gothenburg) from the age of four onward. He was NCAA champion in men's epee in 1978 and led the University of Notre Dame to a first-place team finish the same year. He was World University Games champion in 1981 and won the silver medal at the 1984 Olympics. He earned a Master of Science degree from Chalmers University in Göteborg. While still an active fencer, he began a career in management with Volvo. In 1999, he started his own management consultant firm, Vigor Management AB, which counts Volvo among its many clients. He lives in Göteborg with his wife Ann and their two children.

Ruggero Ceci

Born in Stockholm in 1956, Ruggero began fencing in 1974 and became Johan's teammate at Stockholm's FFF club. He competed at the national level in Sweden in all three weapons, later specializing in epee, and was a member of the Swedish epee team at Heidenheim in 1981. He is now a research psychologist, specializing in the psychophysics of exercise and fatigue in areas including automobile traffic safety, driver impairment, sports education, human factors and human – machine interaction. He is employed by the Swedish Road Administration, where a recent project has involved him in studying the safety of mobile phones in traffic.

Geoff Pingree

Geoff was born and raised in Concord, New Hampshire. In his senior year in high school, he signed up for a fencing class, beat the other student, and declared himself Concord's champion. He entered MIT in 1976 and eventually became IFA individual epee champion and an NCAA All-America. He also worked with Coach Eric Sollee on stage fighting and went from fight choreography to acting for the Shakespeare Ensemble. (He still acts, directs and designs for the theater.) He received an architecture degree from Harvard and is currently an architect in the Boston area. He specializes in theatre design and has also contributed to the renovation of the MIT and Harvard fencing rooms.

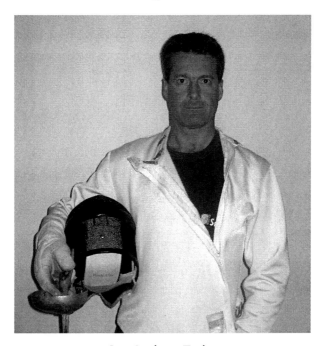

Our Authors Today
Above, Ruggero Ceci; Below, Geoff Pingree

Introduction

It is August 1989, a year of change. The place is the quiet seaside resort town of Hapsal, in what is now the independent republic of Estonia, but was then part of the Soviet Union. In that same month, two million people joined hands to form a human chain stretching across Estonia, Latvia, and Lithuania, the three Baltic republics of the Soviet Union – a harbinger of its imminent collapse. I had expressed an interest in visiting the area from my native Sweden to observe the indigenous Swedish-speaking people there who had survived occupation by both Nazi Germany and Stalin's Soviet Union. I was somewhat surprised when I received an invitation to visit this area, closed to Westerners for 50 years. Despite being semi-retired from top-level competition, I was also there for the Hapsal epee tournament that attracted fencers from all over the USSR and its satellite states. (Estonia was one of the leading fencing centers outside Moscow.)

I was surprised to see that during my absence, the distinctive (and classical) Soviet fencing style had vanished. All 150 fencers present in the stadium used a style that clearly reminded me of my own: constant bouncing, close distance, lots of infighting, simple actions. Boris Lukomski, possibly the best Soviet epeeist never to have won the World Championship, was standing next to me. He read my mind and said in his good English: "Isn't it terrible – and it's all your fault. You and the Germans."

I decided at that moment to write this book.

Boris was right: something dramatic had happened to epee fencing (as well as to foil and to a lesser extent to sabre) starting in the 1970's. Modern fencing strategy had developed from 1973 onward and was more or less matured by 1980 (but was not yet adopted by all nations). I had been in the middle of this process, winning the World Championship in 1977 and the Olympic Games in 1980. This strategy still rules the fencing pistes around the world. I feel strongly that there is an untold story to tell.

Despite being undeniably effective, the modern fencing paradigm remains bitterly controversial. Some argue (correctly) that classical fencing has disappeared: its distinct and sometimes complex fencing phrases executed at the right time (the conversation of blades) have been replaced by a physical form of fencing with very few precise phrases and certainly no complex moves. The new approach employs speed and distance as its critical elements, meaning that what previously was thought of as "fencing talent" is no longer needed for success – at least, not to anything like the same extent.

As I will describe later in the book, my own fencing talent (in the former sense) was not enough for success, and so I was forced to create a new style simply to make me successful. It was not my intention to make classical fencing obsolete but this was the unfortunate consequence. I would like to add in my defense that the Soviets had already moved away from classical fencing as early as the 1960's.

Even though telling the story of how the new style emerged is probably strong enough motivation for writing this book, it is certainly not the only reason. Fencing literature is extensive. Coaches, many without world-class experience, have written most of this literature. The few books written by world-class fencers are worth reading, even if they are old (see The Living Sword and On Fencing by Aldo Nadi[1]). Most books written by coaches describe classical fencing, which is now obsolete in world-class competition – and these books are sufficient for beginners. They describe movements and exercises, sometimes hundreds of them, which can be used for training students. But even if you learn all of them, you may still not win a match. There is a gap between performing exercises and using movements to actually win.

---

[1] Aldo Nadi, *The Living Sword*, (Sunrise, Florida: Laureate Press, 1995), and *On Fencing*, (Sunrise, Florida: Laureate Press, [1943] 1996).

Furthermore, most fencing literature concentrates on foil (and to a lesser extent on sabre), but little is found specializing in the old dueling weapon, the epee[1]. This means that there is a discrepancy between what is taught by fencing masters (hundreds of complicated movements) and the reality in world-class epee, where only simple movements are used (even a action like a disengage is not very common in a World Championship final). Is there a reason? Are there lessons to be learned? I would answer, yes. This book is an attempt to bridge the current gaps between theory and practice, and describe as clearly as possible one epee-fencing paradigm for winning.

I use the word "paradigm" to emphasize that it is the thinking behind winning that is important and that this thinking can be utilized with a number of different moves. Therefore, this book is different. It will concentrate on the thinking rather than the possible moves. The word paradigm will thus be used as the term to describe the overall approach. The paradigm can include a strategy that is particular for a specific fencer, but it remains independent of specific opponents and the tactics that are specific for each opponent, each bout and sometimes each hit (if a fencer elects to change tactics during the bout). It is important to try to use clear terminology, but it should be understood that there is a significant overlap between the connected terms paradigm – strategy – tactics. In reality they may often be used interchangeably.

This book is demanding. I will assume that the average reader has been fencing for five years or so, has the ability to perform most of the classical fencing moves, and understands the reasons behind them. If you have fenced less than that, do not expect to understand everything and do not attempt to use all the ideas discussed in this book. Instead, you should still be concentrating

---

[1] Many fencing handbooks reduce epee to a brief chapter. Imre Vass's *Epee Fencing: A Complete System* (Staten Island, NY: SKA SwordPlay Books, 2003 [Hungarian original 1965]) is an example of a purely classical approach that lists more than 100 possible actions. See Roger Crosnier's *Fencing With the Epee: Instruction and Technique* (New York: A. S. Barnes, 1958) for a fine handbook from the classical point of view and Terence Kingston's *Epee Combat Manual* (UK: Terence Kingston, 2001) for a very concise modern approach.

on learning the wide variety of techniques that comprise classical fencing. This book can provide you with directions for your long journey to fencing expertise – as well as an understanding of why you lose to better fencers! It is nice to know where you may be heading, and why. Still, fencing remains complex, so please use your common sense – and listen to your coach.

There is one more reason for me to write this book – and for you to read it.

Most world-class fencers in my time were both classically trained and very competitive. They were already leaders at the junior level and so did not need to bother themselves by thinking about all the details that made them win (or lose); they just succeeded naturally. My career, however, was atypical. Even though I trained very hard, I did not have enough "fencing talent" to win with the classical fencing style I had been taught. I always lost when I tried to fence classically and I was never a good junior. My route to winning required me to understand my weaknesses and to design a style that compensated for them. I had to even out the natural advantages that my opponents had. I had to figure out all the details that most other fencers did not need to think about.

As a result, I can now tell others about this process. Therefore, this book contains advice and directions for those like me, who can't win "naturally" and whose fencing is forced into a different dimension. This new dimension has its own demands that will decide who wins and who loses, but at least you can prepare for them. A layman's description of this new approach is that it is a way to "kill" – or at least neutralize – fencing talent.

Early in this book, I give a simplified description of the new paradigm. In the following chapters of the book, I try to make the presentation as clear as possible. Chapter 6 describes the various parts of the paradigm in more detail and acknowledges the contributions of others. The rest of the book will describe the consequences of the paradigm from different points of view.

One more note: for simplicity, I have chosen to describe a fencer using the pronoun "he," even though I know that there are many female fencers. One of the virtues of fencing is that male and female fencers always train and sometimes compete together. I ask forgiveness if I have unintentionally offended any reader.

The MIT foil team with the Little Iron Man trophy, 1974. From left: MIT men's coach Silvio Vitale, fencers Arlie Sterling, Johan Harmenberg, and Rich Reimer, and coach Eric Sollee. See the next chapter for the story of how the MIT foil team, went from underdogs to IFA champions after beginning to explore Eric Sollee's Three Conjectures.

1.

Background and a Meeting

Sun-tzu said:
[The factors that] enable the masses of the Three
Armies invariably to withstand the enemy without be-
ing defeated are the unorthodox (ch'i) and the orthodox
(cheng).
In general, in battle one engages with the orthodox
and gains victory through the unorthodox. Thus one who
excels at sending forth the unorthodox is as inexhaust-
ible as Heaven, as unlimited as the Yangtze and Yellow
river.
... In warfare the strategic configurations of power
(shih) do not exceed the unorthodox and orthodox, but
the changes of the unorthodox and orthodox can never be
completely exhausted. The unorthodox and orthodox mu-
tually produce each other, just like an endless cycle. Who
can exhaust them?[1]

I started fencing in September, 1966 at the age of 11 in my
native city of Stockholm, Sweden. After one term of practicing
only three times a week, I started training daily. My coach was

---

[1] From Sun-tzu, *Art of War*, tr. Ralph D. Sawyer, (Boulder, Colorado: West-
view Press, 1994.) Sun-tzu's *Art of War* ranks with Clausewitz's *On War* as the
world's most famous and influential study of strategy. It is dated to the Spring
and Autumn period of the Eastern Chou Dynasty of the 6th Century BC.
   The Eastern tradition has two different entities for "unorthodox" and "orthodox" (ch'i and cheng), whereas in the Western tradition, one is simply the
negative of the other. Eastern traditions always mention unorthodox before
orthodox, whereas the opposite is true for Western traditions. Note that the
unorthodox when widely used will become the norm and thus the orthodox.
The entities therefore mutually produce each other in "an endless cycle," as
Sun-Tzu writes.

Rudolf Meckel, a well-educated fencing master from Austria. His view was that the "art of fencing" was more important than the "art of winning," and consequently all his students had to spend considerable time practicing weapon movements without an opponent. Meckel (as he preferred to be called) decided when the student was ready to start actual training bouts. I fenced my first bout only after more than two years of "dry" (non-electric, or "steam") fencing, and I was more fortunate than some who went as many as three years before facing an opponent. We all fenced foil, since Meckel believed foil to be the ideal weapon for practicing classical weapon phrases. Of course I fenced with a French grip, holding it the classical way (with my thumb tight inside the guard, next to the pad). Epee was tolerated but not encouraged, but after more than 5 years of fencing, I made epee my first priority. I received a thorough drilling in classical technique and totally embraced the ideals included in the "art of fencing." It is an irony of fate that I, who most completely embraced the art of classical fencing, was destined to destroy those ideals.

The only important difference between Meckel and most of the other classical fencing masters was a strong emphasis on speed, both in the movement of the weapon and leg-foot speed. He demanded tough speed training exercises and made us jump rope daily. This emphasis proved valuable to me later.

During these years, I had some modest success at foil. Still, after seven years of intense training and competition in both foil and epee, I realized that I did not have the technique needed to become a good national-level junior fencer, let alone an international competitor. So during my senior year of high school, I decided to change directions and give up my competitive ambitions. (I still had a deep love for fencing and fenced for fun.)

Luckily, I did not give up my academic ambitions and consequently did well in school. I was attracted by computer science, and the US was the place to study that, even though America was then a backwater as far as fencing was concerned. I applied to two universities and was admitted to both of them. One was Yale, but I was unable to find New Haven on my map. I was able to find Boston, so I chose the Massachusetts Institute of Technology (MIT), which was fortunately located in Cambridge, Massachusetts, just outside Boston proper. Great effects were to flow from this almost random decision.

During my first week at MIT in August 1973, there was an athletic fair when different sports tried to attract new students. I naturally drifted towards the fencers. They seemed to be a nice bunch. However, Head Coach Silvio Vitale brusquely informed me that the beginners' courses started in November. After failing to persuade him that I was not a beginner, I tried to explain that I wanted to fence right away. He told me that this was also impossible, and I wondered what a strange place I had ended up in. I was totally unaware of the NCAA[1] rule that the university could not sponsor a sport outside its designated season. It is still surprising to me that nobody took the trouble to explain these rules at the time.

Coach Vitale finally asked me which weapon I fenced. I explained that epee was my best weapon, but that I also fenced some foil. He said, "Good. We need a foil fencer." Luckily, there were other fencing freshmen at the fair, Arlie Sterling and Rich Reimer. They also seemed to be ignorant about the rules, so we decided to fence on our own, even though it was obvious that MIT did not want us to. To protect the innocent and the not so innocent, I will not describe how we freshmen got access to the necessary equipment and fencing venue.

When I gave up competitive fencing, I also changed to an orthopedic (pistol) grip and I started using this at MIT. The immediate result was that for some reason my best parry, fourth, didn't work the way it had before. This had been the strong point of my game. (I never recovered it, with a partial exception that I shall come to later.) Therefore, I was severely disadvantaged, fencing with the "wrong" weapon and with my favorite parry gone. I had

[1] The National Collegiate Athletic Association (NCAA) is the US association that governs university sports. "Student-athletes" must be amateurs (or at least appear to be); and they are not allowed to practice their sport at their college or university out of its designated season. The rules have not changed in this regard since 1973.

to ask myself: was it possible to win without a complete game? Was it possible to win with no or little bladework?

We three freshmen trained together more or less daily during that first quarter of the academic year and developed a style that was increasingly based on speed. When the other fencers at last started practicing in November, they stood no chance. The FFF (Fabulous Freshmen Foil team) won most competitions that academic year, including the oldest intercollegiate tournament, the Little Iron Man trophy of the Intercollegiate Fencing Association. This tournament predated the NCAA national championship and at that time was a tougher contest. Clearly, it was possible to win bouts without a complete game – at least at the American college level of that time.

When fencing started in November, I met the person who was to change my fencing career, Eric Sollee, the MIT women's fencing coach. I will let Geoff Pingree, who also enjoyed success as a student of Eric's at MIT, tell Eric's story up to the time our life paths crossed.

1.1 Geoff Pingree: Eric Sollee's Background

Born in California in 1926, Eric found himself as a teenager in the Philippines shortly before the war. There he noticed Japanese fifth columnists – pretending to be farmers – practicing with their samurai swords. His family was to be caught in the Japanese occupation and, as American citizens, spent the war in an internment camp. Here, as a teenager, Eric took up boxing, whose principles would always remain with him as he developed his fencing.

After the war was over, Eric, now old enough to join the military, signed up and served in Korea. Here, during some time off, he acted as a boxing coach for some of his fellow soldiers. One of them, a poor boxing student as Eric remembers him, was having difficulty with the sport. As Eric explained some of the principles to him, the student's eyes lit up. "That sounds like fencing," he said.

"What's that?" Eric asked, and his awkward boxing student responded by performing a swift and fluid lunge. Eric became fascinated with the sport. He attempted to find out as much as he could about fencing, but his friend insisted that he wait until he got back to the States to get proper training. Eric, who had been serving in the army in order to qualify for tuition from the GI Bill, had been admitted to Harvard, which had a very good fencing program. It is strange to think of, but also characteristic of Eric's life, that he would be exposed to this most European of sports while in the Far East.

At Harvard, René Peroy, a French-trained former champion, offered a rigorous training in foil. Because of Eric's lack of experience in fencing when he arrived at Harvard, Peroy kept his training very simple, emphasizing the mastery of only a few moves. Peroy would often strap Eric's foot to the floor so that he could not move while he gave him a lesson in order to force him to master his parries. Eric eventually developed into one of Harvard's top fencers. In Eric's senior year, Peroy decided that he needed a stronger sabre fencer for the team and moved Eric over to that weapon, again training him rigorously in a few simple moves. While foil remained Eric's best weapon, his training in sabre, a much more mobile and dynamic game, was to be another important influence on him.

After leaving Harvard, Eric moved to New York City, the center of fencing in the United States. Here he joined the prestigious and competitive New York Athletic Club, received lessons from Odon Niederkirchner and was able to fence consistently with the best fencers in the country. Like Eric, Niederkirchner also had experience as a boxer and the two of them would compare various aspects of the two martial arts.

This was the period when electronic scoring equipment was being introduced in foil. (Epee had been fenced electrically since 1936; foil became electric at the 1956 Olympics.) This was a paradigm shift that split the fencing community into advocates of the old and the new styles of fencing. The right of way rules and reliance on human side judges to decide if a touch had been scored had long constrained fencing to old interpretations of what constituted a valid fencing action: it was not enough for a touch to hit; it had to be seen to hit. Electronic scoring allowed more freedom for the competitive fencer. Eric was an early advocate of a new school of thought that tried to take advantage of the new possibilities. This paradigm shift helped prepare Eric for the shift in thinking that occurred when he and Johan started reinterpreting fencing strategy.

His life took several other turns. One was a return to the Philippines for several years. Here he not only continued to fence, but also had some exposure to different martial arts in the form of eskrima or kali (Filipino stick fighting) and judo. As with his boxing experience, Eric would always be taking note of possible lessons that could be drawn from other martial arts and how they could be applied to fencing.

Eventually he returned to the States and ended up back in New England, where his wife was pursuing her education. Here he became involved with a unique project at the Carroll Center for the Blind. Fencing instruction was being given to the blind students there in order to help them become more sensitive to space and improve their mobility. This presented Eric with a whole new way of thinking about coaching (I remember occasionally taking lessons from Eric while I was blindfolded). This lent a strong neurological science perspective to his ideas of fencing.

Eric's unique experiences, his background in boxing, the influence of eastern martial arts, his rigorous classical fencing training with Peroy and Niederkirchner, his own observations of the potential of new thinking when electronic scoring was introduced and his development of a fencing program for the blind all gave him distinctive perspective on the sport of fencing.

Back in the Boston area, Eric continued to fence and to train himself as a coach. He was learning from both Edo Marion, Harvard's fencing master, and Silvio Vitale, the MIT coach. This was a unique environment in which to practice. The science and engineering mind-set of MIT opened up unique pathways and fresh insights into old paradigms.

1.2 Johan: the Three Conjectures

When I came to MIT, I was an heir to a western tradition of classical fencing knowledge developed over hundreds of years. This tradition focuses on one basic question: What can I do to hit my opponent? In short, *a total focus on yourself.* Eric brought a Japanese tradition, also developed over centuries, which asks a different set of questions: What does your opponent want to do? What is the status of his soul? Is he scared? Is he brave? Is he about to do something foolish? Hence, *a total focus on your opponent.*

It has always surprised me that many coaches claim to have the final answer to most technical and strategic fencing questions. They also claim that there are good or bad moves and that a good move is good for all fencers and in all situations. These coaches seldom get involved with their fencers outside the club and insist that fencers should pay them exaggerated and outdated respect. Clearly, this type of coach will not contribute to the future development of fencing.

Eric Sollee was different. His experience of Japanese martial arts made him humble in his approach to fencing and gave him the understanding that both fencers in a bout will decide whether a particular move is good or bad in a very simple manner: a good move scores and a bad move does not. He also had a clear understanding that all fencers need an individual strategy for training and competitions, covering lessons, technique and style. Sollee's coaching approach is dramatically different for each fencer and is based on a substantial, frequent and open exchange of ideas between coach and student. Finally, he encourages his students to focus their attention on their opponent and his possibilities rather than on themselves.

After fencing, we often ended up at the Fathers IV, a friendly bar on 300 Massachusetts Avenue near MIT. One evening Eric suggested that we could ask the essential questions from the point of view of the Japanese tradition of martial arts, but address them with the tools and thinking of the western tradition of fencing. I do not think that any of us present that evening understood the revolutionary consequences of this approach.

During our discussions in 1973, our main topic was the possibility of designing a new fencing style based on speed and little blade contact. Sollee and his team formulated the three questions that had to be answered to make a new style possible. The three unknowns, called the Sollee Conjectures, were initially written on the back of a paper table napkin (I had the original napkin for some time but it is now long gone).

Classical fencing had assumed that the fencer with superior technique would control the outcome, that the fencer who maintained the longer distance had the advantage, and that the key to victory lay in defeating the opponent's best moves. To some extent, this paradigm is still taught, and believed, today. In fact, it remains valid when both fencers are fencing *within the classical paradigm*. Eric's conjectures proposed nothing less than standing this paradigm on its head.

Sollee's conjectures:

1.   Is it possible for the fencer with the lower technical fencing ability to decide the technical level of a bout?

2.   Can the fencer with the shorter fencing distance control the distance in a bout?

3.   Is it possible to force your opponent into you own area of greatest strength – which we later called your AoE?

The possibilities seemed exciting. And since I had renounced my serious fencing ambitions, I had nothing to lose. I volunteered to totally re-engineer my fencing style for full-scale testing. The next day the team began to experiment with the new possibilities.

Now, more than 30 years later, the answer to all three questions is clearly yes, and the answers have passed the test of time with honor.

The Sollee Conjectures:

1. Is it possible for the fencer with the lower technical fencing ability to decide the technical level of a bout?

2. Can the fencer with the shorter fencing distance control the distance in a bout?

3. Is it possible to force your opponent into your own area of greatest strength?

2.

The New Paradigm

Sun-tzu said:

"In antiquity those that excelled in warfare first made themselves unconquerable in order to await [the moment when] the enemy could be conquered.

"Being unconquerable lies with yourself; being conquerable lies with the enemy.

"Thus one who excels in warfare is able to make himself unconquerable, but cannot necessarily cause the enemy to be conquerable.

"Thus it is said a strategy for conquering the enemy can be known but yet not possible to implement.

2.1 A Sketch of the New Paradigm

To introduce the new paradigm in its developed form, let us begin with its departure from the classical fencing paradigm.

Suppose that your opponent would like to make an attack by step forward – feint into the fourth line – disengage lunge into the sixth line. This very basic attack is based on a number of assumptions. We will later use the term "hidden prerequisites (HP's) to describe what he must assume:

- You will be at normal or long fencing distance;
- You will take the right parry at the right distance (if you take a late parry, there will be no room to disengage);
- You will stand still (fixed back foot) or retreat in a controlled way;
- You will not do anything unpredictable.

The classical or orthodox answer to your opponent's planned attack is for you to go along with his intentions and at the end take one extra parry – for example, a fourth followed by a sixth, or a different parry from the one expected – for example, first or a ninth. (The latter option assumes significant guesswork.)

The new paradigm suggests that an equally valid, or even a better, alternative is to deny your opponent the hidden prerequisites for his action, making all of his assumptions wrong:

- *Shorten the distance* so your opponent does not have the space or time to disengage or advance-lunge.
- *Take no parry at all* so that no disengage is possible – your opponent's disengage ends in the closed sixth line.
- *Move forward instead of standing still* or retreating, so as to prevent your opponent from executing a step forward – disengage.

Sun Tzu's 2500-year-old statement at the head of this chapter summarizes my own view of fencing strategy. You can and should make it very difficult for the opponent to score. You can and should destroy his game. "But this alone is not enough to win. As Sun Tzu said, "One who excels in warfare is able to make himself unconquerable, but cannot necessarily cause the enemy to be conquerable." You need something more. As I will argue later in the book, this something more is forcing the opponent into making a mistake.

This would make you invulnerable to your opponent's planned attack, which is Sun-tzu's first priority. Let us now assume that we somehow make ourselves invulnerable, not just to this one attack, but from most of the possibilities available to an opponent. This increases the possibilities that he ends up playing into our own strength, which we will later call our Area of Excellence (AoE). Thus he "makes himself conquerable." To make ourselves invulnerable, unconquerable, and to cause the opponent make himself vulnerable, conquerable – these are the key elements of the new paradigm.

Let us now explore this new paradigm in more detail.

2.2 A Little More Depth

First, some basics.

How predictable is a fencing bout? A casual observer might conclude that it is totally unpredictable. There are hundreds (or thousands) of different valid fencing movements and variations thereof. Each of them has a variety of valid responses. Each individual fencer has preferences, but we still end up with a vast number of possible combinations. Any one of them can be chosen at any moment, so it should be very difficult to predict a sequence.

But let us ask the question a different way: Suppose you have qualified for an Olympic final. How will you be feeling?

Some writers have described the feelings of some top athletes immediately before an Olympic final as that of "joyful anticipation." But these studies were not about fencing. Fencing is one of the few sports where there is a direct mind-to-mind confrontation, and which includes hundreds of different valid alternative actions for both fencers.

Fencers rarely admit that they are nervous, but what actually happens in a bout that decides an Olympic medal? One clue is this: my experience of a number of world-class finals is that the quality of fencing is much lower than in other situations. Fencers who claim never to be nervous will be nervous for the first time in their lives in an Olympic final, whether they admit it to themselves or not. People rarely admit they are nervous.

I do not have that problem, since I am always nervous. I can even be nervous in practice. If I am unprepared and somebody suggests that the loser of the next bout will buy the winner a beer, I will always lose. This makes me all too familiar with the feeling of nervousness, so I know exactly how to handle it when correctly prepared. This is naturally a competitive advantage for me in a final.

It is a fact that the fencing in an Olympic final is of lower quality, more stereotypical and more predictable than in qualification rounds or the finals of lesser competitions. This can only be explained by psychological factors and for simplicity I will call these factors "nervousness."

I would describe my own feelings as a combination of the joyful anticipation that writers talk about ... and incapacitating nervousness.

So you, too, will be nervous, as will be your opponent. You think about – or you feel – all your years of training. You think about – or you feel – all your friends and relatives who have helped you over the years and who are watching you in person or on television. You think about – or you feel – the pressure of the media, who are there to find out whether you are made of the right stuff.

Maybe you are, maybe you are not.

The pressure is so intense that it is impossible to describe. I guarantee that all the fencers in an Olympic final have these thoughts (and many others) in their heads when they take the few but heavy steps towards the final piste.

And the last thing that you see and hear before you go on to the piste is your coach, who is so nervous that the advice he throws at you is incoherent!

Let us ask this Olympic finalist what his dream scenario will be for this ultimate bout – what would he like his opponent to do and how does he want to respond? There is no such thing as a sure touch. There are only probabilities of risk and chance and he would like to stack the cards in his favor. He wants to maximize his chance of scoring while at the same time minimizing the risk of being hit.

Let us assume that his dream scenario is that the opponent will extend his arm so that our fencer can then make his favorite move: sixth parry with a bind riposte. Our fencer will almost certainly try this parry-riposte if given the opportunity, because it is his preferred move under pressure. He cannot stop himself.

My experience is that at least 95% of top fencers will perform only their favorite move if given the opportunity. And most fencers will be even more predictable in an Olympic final. Many of them will even be so nervous that they will attempt their favorite movements even though the prerequisites are not totally perfect. In other words, they will make mistakes.

Let us call a fencer's dream action his "area of excellence" or AoE. (Actually, I regard fencing as multi-dimensional, so "volume" would be more accurate than "area." But I'll stick to "area" because most people find it clearer.) This fencer will use his AoE if given the opportunity in an Olympic final. In fact, he'll use it in any situation where he wants desperately to win, when making the next hit is more important than anything else at that particular moment.

I think all experienced fencers will recognize this situation. Let us call these very important hits "Olympic touches." They will appear in a number of different situations, not just the Olympics. Suppose that Harvard meets Columbia in an intercollegiate team match. The score is 13-all when the last bout starts. I guarantee that the fencers will feel the same as they would in an Olympic final, so the hits in the match qualify as Olympic touches from a mental pressure perspective.

Olympic touches are more predictable than other hits and appear in many situations where both fencers feel desperate to score the next hit. Because they are more predictable, Olympic touches should be handled differently from other hits. It is obvious that if you have the superior strategy in handling the important touches, you will have a superior chance of winning your bouts. So let us concentrate on the Olympic touches. As for me, during my 4 years as a top international competitor, I can only remember losing one important last-hit situation (at 4-all in a 5-touch bout or 9-all in the 10-touch bouts that were standard for direct elimination tournaments in my time), counting both individual competitions and team events. I was a nightmare for my opponents.

The rest of this book will describe a strategy for handling these Olympic touches. Ordinary training and ordinary lessons are not sufficient preparation.

2.3 Handling Olympic Touches

There are three main ways to handle Olympic touches in relation to your opponent's AoE: trying to fence outside both fencers' AoE, trying to defeat your opponent's AoE, and fencing within your own AoE.

A. Fencing outside both fencers' AoE.

This is by definition unpredictable, since it is outside both fencers' charted territory. The fencer with the best classical training should win, and usually did before the mid-1960's, when the Russians introduced their style based on simplicity, strength, length and speed. An inexperienced fencer who has by chance ended up in an Olympic touch situation might increase his chances of winning from nearly nothing to something by using the highly unpredictable nature of this approach.

B. Trying to defeat your opponent's AoE.

This naturally makes the fencing much more predictable, assuming that you have analyzed your opponent properly. You know, for example, that your opponent wants to take a sixth parry followed by a bind riposte, and that you give him the opportunity of doing this. Since you can anticipate his reaction, you might try to disengage and hit him as he tries his parry-riposte. This approach is perfectly valid but contains a number of prerequisites. Since your opponent decides when to take his parry (early or late), deceiving his parry with a disengage requires a lot of classical fencing talent and training. Besides, your opponent may anticipate your action and take a fourth parry instead.

The problem with this approach is therefore threefold:

1. It requires a high level of classical fencing talent and superior technical skills.

2. It allows your opponent many possible attractive alternatives. He gets to decide how and when to *begin* actions that will lead to a hit – on him or you or both, and he also gets to make the *final* decision to commit (FDC).

3. Because you are fencing in your opponent's AoE, he will by now have analyzed the possibilities and alternatives – and practiced for this exact situation – much better than you can possibly have done.

[A note on the FDC is in order here.

In top fencing, the fencers normally move around until Fencer 1 decides on (commits to) a final action in such a way that it will irreversibly lead to a touch – whether by him, his opponent, or both. He can no longer change his mind. But now Fencer 2 gets the opportunity – and the advantage – either to decline the action totally through blocking or retreating or to execute whatever counteraction will increase his changes of scoring. It should be noted that in this example, Fencer 2, not Fencer 1, gets the FDC.]

To return to our example: if you (as Fencer 1) extend your arm to make OP take his sixth parry, OP has a number of options. He can take his parry while retreating, moving forwards, or standing still. You may be successful once, but your opponent will rapidly learn, so that you cannot easily succeed again, at least not in the same bout. Finally, although *you* are in an Olympic touch situation, your opponent may not be. That means he may feel free to do something completely outside his preferred AoE, like extend into your extension. Now, because you are waiting for a parry, he might hit you.

And even if your opponent is in an Olympic touch situation, because you are fencing in your opponent's AoE, he will by now have analyzed the possibilities and alternatives – and practiced for this exact situation – much better than you can possibly have done.

Trying to defeat your opponent's AoE can therefore be characterized as resulting in predictable fencing but is risky and requires a lot of technical fencing talent.

Ironically, many coaches advise their students to use exactly this approach as they go on to the piste for an important bout: "When your opponent takes his favorite sixth parry, just disengage!" My advice in the same situation would be, "Make sure that your opponent never, ever gets the chance to take that sixth parry."

C. Fencing inside your own AoE.

This fencing paradigm was pioneered be Eric Sollee and his team at MIT in 1973, although elements were already found in Soviet fencing during the 1960's.

This is the reverse of the previous approach. If you have, as most fencers do (including me), a defensive AoE, you will have the tremendous advantage of the FDC, the final decision to commit. You will be the one who gets the opportunity to decide when and how the final fencing phrases that irreversibly lead to scoring will be performed. (You can, of course, decline any action by retreating away from the invitation.)

Naturally, you will try to stack the deck so that the possibilities of hitting outweigh the risks of being hit. Because you control your own AoE, you can analyze all your opponent's options because they are not too many. You can train and prepare for *every possible action* that might occur within your own AoE. It is obvious that you give away the element of surprise, but in return you get greatly increased predictability – both of the action itself and of its outcome. In addition, you retain the FDC. Of course, it requires a lot of targeted training to prepare for all your opponent's possibilities within your own AoE.

All well and good, you say, but the critical question remains: is it possible to get your opponent into your own AoE repeatedly? The answer is yes, under certain circumstances. Let's look at Figure 1 on the following page.

2.3.1 Possible reactions to OP's AoE

At the top center of Figure 1 is my opponent's AoE: a bind in fourth.

From the upper left to the lower right of the diagram my possible reactions (assuming that I know my opponent's preference) are arranged in order of the level of classical technique required to execute them.

My actions may be intended to *score a hit*, or they may be designed *to avoid being hit*. The actions that are designed to score require more technical skill and accordingly are to the left of the diagram, separated by a heavy diagonal bar from those that are designed to avoid the touch.

1) I can attack in my own tempo (on my initiative) in order to preempt the action, but then I will probably wind up inside my opponent's AoE, his preferred fourth bind.

2) I can allow his bind and attempt to hit him by one of the following:

Epee 2.0

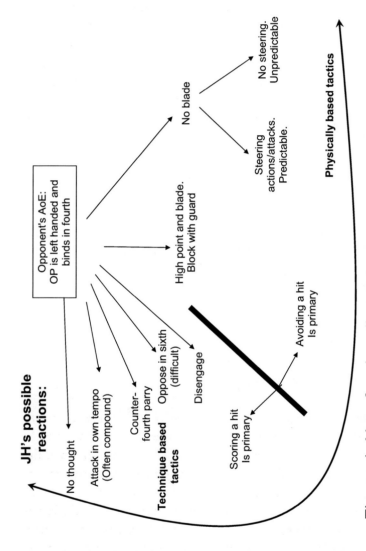

Figure 1: New fencing dimension, list of possible JH reactions on OP's AoE

a)   Counter-fourth parry to control his blade,

b)   Sixth opposition to regain control,

c)   Disengage and attempt to hit.

But in all these cases, I am still within my opponent's AoE, because these are the classical answers to my opponent's taking of my blade; hence he has anticipated them and practiced dealing with them. Even if I am successful once, I have no assurance of repeating my success. I will be playing the classical chess game inside my opponent's favored territory, or else I will simply be guessing, with completely unpredictable results.

The above actions, to the left and above the diagonal bar, are all designed to hit my opponent, require a high level of skill, and fall within my opponent's AoE.

Now, let's look at the actions to the right of the diagonal bar, those that are designed to *avoid being hit.*

3) If I keep my point and blade high, my object is never, ever to let my opponent execute his AoE, *(but to keep him hoping that he'll get the chance, and therefore keep waiting and trying!)*

4) If I keep my arm and blade where he can never get at them (no blade), I have totally removed the prerequisite for his attack, and he has to try a different action altogether.

a) If I'm working to steer him into my own AoE, I don't give him many choices, so the action is somewhat predictable;

b) If I'm not trying to steer him into my AoE, the fencing is much less predictable.

Note that for all these tactics, shortening the distance also limits my opponent's choices. Please also note that fencing with "no blade" tactics requires the fencer to be good at extending the weapon arm when something happens. The weapon arm extension speed is thus a critical success factor for using the "no blade" tactics.

Arranging the possible tactics in descending order of need for classical fencing ability constitutes a new fencing dimension. When one of my fencers is losing a bout, I normally recommend a change of tactics towards the lower right corner, thus removing as many of the opponent's hidden prerequisites as possible. I may also recommend a shorter distance to further limit his choices and thus push the fencing even further towards the lower right corner.

When *both* fencers concentrate on taking away the opponent's hidden prerequisites, the fencing will inevitably end up towards the lower right corner with few classical fencing movements. This is the main reason why even a simple disengage is not common in world-class finals.

3.

The New Paradigm in Action

Let us now get to the core of the thinking that created a new fencing style to deal with Olympic touches. Consider an opponent, OP, a left-handed fencer. OP has the following game plan (his AoE) for Olympic touches: his opponent will extend towards OP's inner or outer upper quadrant: his high lines. Then OP will perform his world-class fourth parry – bind riposte and score the hit.

What possibilities do we have when fencing Olympic touches with OP? (See Figure 1.) We could perform independent actions and hopefully force OP into doing actions outside his AoE. This option is discussed in 2.3 as *"A. Fencing outside both fencers' AoE."* The problem is that OP will not make any attacks by himself unless he can use his favorite fourth bind. Therefore, we need to attack in our own time (our own tempo), irrespective of OP's actions. These attacks will often be compound, and it may be difficult to avoid ending in OP's high lines. Clearly, they can be performed, but require a total technical superiority and are always unpredictable. We do not know what OP will do and cannot exclude the possibility that he might actually manage to perform his favorite parry-riposte. A further problem is that OP might learn after being deceived once.

So it might be better to let OP take his fourth parry, but under circumstances that give us the opportunity to hit him. This is what I mentioned in 2.3 as *"B. Trying to defeat opponent's AoE."* I have listed three possibilities in Figure 1 (there are others). After OP has taken his parry, you wait for his bind riposte and take his blade with an action that we call counter of fourth parry and then hit him with a counter-riposte. Or you oppose his bind with a sixth parry-riposte. Finally, you can disengage when OP tries his fourth parry. All these options have one thing in common: they require a high level of technical skill – probably superior to that of OP. They require classical fencing talent of a high order.

These actions also still have as their primary focus to the aim of hitting OP. Consequently, sooner or later you will need to give OP your blade, and thus potentially falling within his AoE. Finally, these actions focus on your own intentions. They represent the classical response to a fencing problem. Note that the actions labeled "*B. Attempting to defeat opponent's AoE*" do not necessarily guarantee actually hitting OP. Because you are fencing well within his AoE, he is probably perfectly aware of your options and knows exactly how to handle your responses. He has most probably trained to handle them.

Let us now change the perspective and focus on OP with the primary objective of avoiding being hit. What options do we have now? First we need to clearly define the prerequisites for OP's AoE. His only prerequisite is binding the blade. Can we fence without ever giving him the blade? The answer is yes. Three options are listed in Figure 1 (there are others). You can fence with a high blade and a high point. I mean *really* high! Your point should be higher than OP's mask and pointing upwards. This should give OP no real chance to bind the blade, but it might tempt him into trying – after all, it is his favorite move. Of course this attempt will fail if we are successful with our tactics.

Another option is total absence of blade. You can point your blade towards the floor, to the left or right of him anywhere outside his reach, even if he starts his AoE. With these tactics, you are signaling to OP that he will never, ever have the opportunity to perform his favorite move. The no-blade tactics will force OP either to do nothing or to make attacks without using his favorite move. If OP performs an attack without binding in fourth , it will by definition be outside his AoE and might end up outside your own AoE. This will potentially make the fencing unpredictable.

However, the no-blade tactics contain a variant: you can make certain movements that limit OP's ability to freely decide which attack he would like to perform and when to perform it. These are called *steering actions*: movements that steer your opponent's attack to the area of your own choosing, your own AoE. You can, for example, force your opponent to attack low (or high) according to your own preference.

Finally, you can decide not to perform any steering actions at all, which will make the fencing unpredictable again, with problems that are approaching the situation in 2.3 called *"A. Fencing outside both fencers' AoE"*.

The two options "high point and blade" and "no-blade steering" are the prerequisites for the tactics discussed in 2.3 as "*C. Fencing inside your own AoE*. These actions also require less technical skill than the other actions discussed above. Because the nature of these tactics is to avoid being hit and to prevent OP binding the blade, requirements other than traditional classical fencing are needed. These include physical fitness, good reactions, speed, good nerves and close combat skills. We normally call this approach *physically-based* tactics, in order to separate it from *technique-based* tactics. Back in the 1970's, these physically-based tactics successfully challenged all previous assumptions and fundamentally changed the nature of fencing.

However, one basic question still remains to be answered:

Is it possible to "force" OP into our own AoE, which is the continuation of the "high point and blade" and "no-blade steering" tactics? Before we wrap it all up, we need to consider our own choices.

I will use myself as an example.

When I was a young fencer in Sweden, before I changed my grip from French to pistol at MIT in 1973, the strong point of my game was a very sensitive and fast fourth parry-riposte. (I call it sensitive because I had the ability to let my opponent come very close before actually parrying). However, as I have already mentioned, I lost my fourth parry-riposte totally when I changed to a pistol grip. During the academic year of 1973 – 74, I was mainly fencing foil and did not have any strong point in my blade play at all. I explored the possibility of using speed and distance, with little blade play, as the ultimate weapons in my game. When I did fence epee, I found that it was possible to combine variations of the sixth parry with the speed and distance game in a natural way. After returning to Sweden during the summer of 1974, I developed these variants into my AoE.

My preferred action became (and remains) this: getting my opponent to attack in the high line and taking a traditional sixth parry until my blade approaches the vertical midline. From this point, the parry is combined with a rapid extension of the weapon arm to become a very forceful riposte. When the movement is finished and my arm is completely straight, my guard has moved across to my upper right (I am right-handed) so that my arm and shoulder are protected behind the guard. So it is a parry-riposte in one forward motion. This is always my preferred action.

My opponents have naturally tried to avoid getting into the trap. Sometimes they attack with a half-extended arm, intending to bind my blade in sixth because they are afraid of my sixth parry. In this case it is more difficult to execute my AoE. If I elect to take a sixth anyway we will in most cases meet mid-blade against mid-blade, and my preferred action is difficult but not impossible to perform. In this case, I normally attempt to pressure my opponent's blade back hard in sixth. Because he is attempting a parry – bind, he must press back. Then I suddenly release the blade, disengage, and hit him. What happens to his point then – why doesn't he hit me as I release? Well, during the whole action, I take a couple of steps forward so that his point ends up behind me and constitutes no threat. Finally, when my opponent takes a proper sixth parry, I can perform a simple disengage and hit him.

In short, I want to draw my opponent into making *any action on my sixth* side, so that I can respond in decreasing order of preference with:

a) sixth parry – bind riposte,
b) sixth parry – disengage riposte, or
c) simple disengage.

It should be noted that I do not distinguish defensive from offensive movements from a fencing strategy point of view. I have described my opponent's movements above as attacking. This is just a matter of convenience. In practice, I might just as well move forward in an attack, and when my opponent threatens my sixth side during his retreat, I perform the identical movements described above and continue the attack to score. This is the way I have always trained myself and this is the way I train my students. I try to find movements that can equally well be used in defense and offence. What is of critical importance is that I always make sure that *I have the advantage of the FDC ("Final Decision to Commit."* All of this described in Figure 2, on the following page, which shows my opponent's possible reactions to my AoE.

My AoE naturally has a number of HP's of its own. These are discussed in 6.6, "The Ideal Opponent."

3.1 Possible OP Reactions to My AoE

Figure 1 focuses on the opponent and his AoE, and how we deal with it. It focuses on not getting hit, and steering the opponent into our own AoE. In the new fencing paradigm, this is the crucial discussion. It is far more important than Figure 2, which discusses our opponent's reaction to our AoE and how we deal with that. But we still need to score, and this is the focus of Figure 2.

Let us therefore assume that I have been successful in forcing my opponent into my AoE – to have OP move his blade towards my sixth side: the upper/outer (high outside) quadrant. What happens how? My options are:

a) My favorite sixth parry – bind,

b) Sixth parry – bind with a final disengage (against opponents who try to oppose in sixth), or

c) Disengage (against opponents coming forward with a parry attempt – which is difficult for the opponent, since there is no blade for him to attempt to parry.)

These are listed in descending order of preference. It is nice to know beforehand where my opponent will end up – *regardless of his movements – prior to his final move!*

He has also given me the FDC.

I have again arranged the actions in descending order of the need for classical fencing technique, from the upper left corner

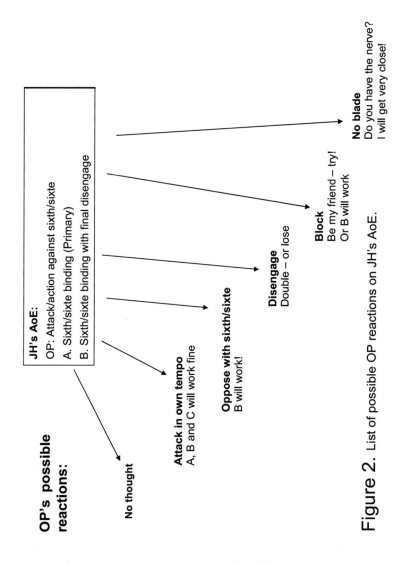

OP's possible reactions:

JH's AoE:
OP: Attack/action against sixth/sixte
A. Sixth/sixte binding (Primary)
B. Sixth/sixte binding with final disengage

No thought

Attack in own tempo
A, B and C will work fine

Oppose with sixth/sixte
B will work!

Disengage
Double – or lose

Block
Be my friend – try!
Or B will work

No blade
Do you have the nerve?
I will get very close!

Figure 2. List of possible OP reactions on JH's AoE.

to the lower right. Since I am forcefully trying to steer my opponent into making attacks into my AoE, some fencers may actually make "attacks in their own tempo" ending up in my AoE. As discussed later, these attacks will often be characterized by *low relative point hit speed*, giving me many alternatives.

All three alternatives listed above are valid, depending on the situation, but a) sixth parry – bind will usually be sufficient.

My opponent may try to "oppose in sixth," which is difficult for him if I am successful in delivering my sixth parry – bind with the intended high relative point hit speed. However, option b) sixth parry – bind followed by a disengage is certainly valid in this case and does not need be decided on beforehand.

A valid tactic from my opponent that happens nearly every bout is that he tries to "disengage" out of my sixth. Since my action, properly executed, involves a lot of forward movement with high relative point hit speed, the best my opponent can hope for is a double touch, unless he is very tall or fences with a French grip held back on the pommel to extend his reach. Normally I score a single hit half the time and a double the rest of the time. When I am in the lead, I often let my opponent disengage in order to have a predictable double.

"Blocking" with the guard (see the cover and frontispiece photo) is often a last resort for fencers seeing no other alternative. Since I have had the privilege of training with Björne Väggö, an expert blocker, for hundreds of hours, I have extensively explored this option. I had three responses in this situation that did not have to be predetermined: fast direct hitting, fast hitting with a late disengage, and, if Björne was successful in blocking, we would enter into a close combat situation. This was a lot of fun since we were both experts at this.

Finally, my opponent might adopt the "no blade" tactics. I would then shorten the distance considerably, which I could do safely because I could usually retreat more quickly and had a faster absolute and relative point hit speed. I would then get closer and closer and wait for my opponent's nerves to break. All actions in Figure 2 are within my AoE and I devoted some 80% of my training to perfecting these actions. So I concentrated on my best features 80% of the time and devoted only 20% to strengthening my weaknesses.

Let's go over these ideas once more.

I have a narrow AoE compared with many other fencers. It is not the size of the AoE that is important; it is the depth and quality. In other words, it is all right to have a narrow AoE, but then it needs to be very, very good. It is normally more important to improve the quality of one's AoE than to expand it. If you want to go down this route, you should devote at least 70% of your training to improving your AoE rather than trying to expand it. *(This advice is for experienced fencers only. You need to learn the full range of fencing moves in order to make an intelligent selection of your AoE.)*

I must assume that my opponent will be aware of my preferred AoE. What are his choices? I have listed some approaches in Figure 2, together with my possible responses. My opponent's most technically advanced strategy is trying to penetrate my defenses with attacks in his own tempo, preferably outside my AoE. He needs to account for my intense attempts to steer his attacks towards my AoE.

But this strategy from my opponent also gives me the possibility of using all of the alternatives within my AoE: sixth parry – bind riposte, sixth parry – disengage riposte, and simple disengage). I am well aware of his approach, since my whole strategy is based on getting my opponent to attack. Naturally, he would like to attack outside my AoE. My job is to make sure his attack lands within my AoE. This will be discussed in a later chapter. The advantage of the FDC resides with me when my opponent uses these tactics.

When I introduced my new strategy during the winter of 1974 – 75, all of my world-class opponents very naturally tried to execute attacks in their own tempo to beat me. They had no success.

It was actually very easy for me.

After a couple of years, especially after I won the World Championship in 1977, few tried this approach any more. Usually, the only exceptions to this rule were a few juniors who felt that they were bound to lose against me if the fencing was too predictable and used the tactics of attacks in their own tempo to increase their chances from nothing to something.

(The other exception was Philippe Riboud. He will be discussed in more detail later on.)

Why didn't my world-class opponents' attacks work? Even world-class fencers generally have only a couple of world-class attacks. After they have shown me these attacks once or twice, I will take precautions to prevent them making them. If they need a certain distance for their attacks, I will be at another distance. If they want to take my blade, I will not give it to them. If they want to attack low, I force them high (into my AoE). For the time being, we can conclude that the strategy of attacking me

- is connected with the need for decisive technical superiority;
- gives away the advantage of FDC,
- is highly unpredictable and,
- even if successful, has a low probability of reproducibility.

In short, this route is unattractive for most fencers.

Other alternatives for my opponent include

A. *Opposing* with a sixth parry (fourth for left-handers) after I have taken my favorite parry – bind riposte. This might work, especially if I timed my riposte badly. My first instinct is to push through an eventual sixth parry against my opponent with speed and strength. I choose specially stiffened and forward-balanced blades to make this happen. If this is not successful, I can make a late disengage, or close the distance and use my superior close-combat fencing skills.[1] Note that this response from my opponent is inside my AoE and I normally train within my AoE 80% of the time. The bottom line is that I am well prepared for this alternative.

---

[1] It was my close-combat fencing skills that ensured I never won any fair-play awards during my college years in the US. I won other awards, though.

B. *Avoiding* my sixth parry – bind by disengaging. This is a perfectly valid alternative that I normally choose to ignore because, if my parry – bind riposte is timed well, the best my opponent can achieve is to get a double. This happens one or twice every match. Half the time I will get a single light and the other half a double. This is also the way I get double hits on purpose. If I have an early lead in a match, I start to make actions with less than optimal timing to encourage my opponent to make a disengage stop hit, which guarantees a double hit and wins me the match. When I am ahead in a match, there is always a danger that my opponent might take unpredictable chances, so it is better to give him a deliberate opening and land a double hit in a predictable manner. Finally, it should be noted that this type of fencing is in the middle of my AoE with the consequences described above.

None of the actions described above is therefore sufficient to be a reliable, reproducible and predictable response to my strategy. What options remain for my opponent then? There are actually two.

C. *Blocking* my sixth parry – bind riposte by holding the guard of the epee slightly higher than shoulder height with an extending arm. My opponent needs to make me do my favorite action without much blade contact in order to have the freedom to block my riposte. My first response is to make a late disengage, but this is highly risky because my opponent's arm is straight or near straight, so his point is right there. My second possibility is to block back and move into close combat. Both of these choices have an unpredictable outcome.

D. Finally, my opponent has the opportunity of *never offering me his blade*. Then I have to get very close to him to force his attacks on me. The vast majority of my matches end up this way, sometimes combined with a blocking attempt when I finally execute my sixth parry – bind riposte. I therefore get a lot of practice with this type of fencing, in which my opponent has more or less copied my strategy.

3.2 Conclusions

Some very interesting conclusions can be drawn from this reasoning.

First, as in Figure 1, the technically demanding strategies – attack in own tempo, oppose with sixth parry-riposte and disengage, and disengage on its own – all focus on scoring, while the other ones focus on avoiding getting hit.

Second, these strategies, which demand decisively superior technical skills, are unattractive to most fencers. They are also unpredictable, since an opponent may learn and may not give the necessary space in time and distance for the technically superior fencer to use his superiority.

Third, the strategy preferred by most fencers – no blade – has extensive similarities with the physically-based tactics described above.

Fourth, within each category of strategy listed in Figure 1 and Figure 2, we have the possibility of varying the distance. A long distance gives more freedom to operate for both fencers and more time to react. A short distance naturally limits the choices and forces the fencing within each category towards the physical tactics extreme. Note that a valid response to an opponent with a very good attack is to close the distance and thereby limit his choices. However, if you decide to use a short fencing distance to limit the choices of your opponent, you need to be aware of what to do ahead of time and you will need a high weapon arm extension speed.

We now have an answer to the first of the Sollee conjectures: Is it possible for the fencer with the lower technical ability to decide the technical level of the bout? Yes, by preventing the more technical fencer from using his superior technique. It takes two to tango.

In addition, we now know why the technical level of world-class epee is so low that even a simple disengage is not common in an Olympic final, as the FIE bitterly complains.

Finally, *all training needs to account for these insights.* Training that simply teaches the moves in the textbooks is not enough.

(N.B. As stated repeatedly in this book, I am only looking at Olympic touches. More technical skills are needed for non-Olympic touches.)

4.

The New Fencing Dimension

To hold down the pillow
"To hold down a pillow" means not allowing the ene-
my's head to rise. ¹
  The important thing in strategy is to suppress the ene-
my's useful actions but allow his useless actions. However,
doing this alone is defensive. First, you must act accord-
ing to the Way, suppress the enemy's techniques, foiling
his plans, and thence command him directly. When you
can do this you will be master of strategy. You must train
well and research "holding down the pillow."
—Miyamoto Musashi²

Fencing can be described as consisting of a number of dimen-
sions. Traditionally, coaches have always tried to explain wins
and losses in different ways. For example, lack of speed ("You
were too slow, or your parry was too slow. Please train more,

---

¹ *To hold down a pillow*: Note that samurai and Japanese ladies slept with their
heads on a small wooden pillow shaped to accommodate their hairstyle.

² From *The Fire Book* in *A Book of Five Rings* by Miyamoto Musashi. Translated by Victor Harris, (Woodstock, NY: The Overlook Press, 1974.) Miyamoto
Musashi was a Japanese samurai, born 1584. He fought his first duel at the age
of 13. He spent most of his life with a ferocious single-mindedness search-
ing for enlightenment by the Way of the Sword. In his Warrior Pilgrimage he
fought 60 duels before the age of 30, winning all. He participated in six wars.
Concerned only with perfecting his skills, "he lived as men need not live, wan-
dering over Japan soaked by the cold winds of winter, not dressing his hair, nor
taking a wife, nor following any profession save his study." It is said he never
entered a bathtub lest he was caught unawares without a weapon, and that his
appearance was uncouth and wretched. At the age of 50 he reached the end of
his search for the Way of the Sword. He then wrote *A Book of Five Rings*, 1645.
The citation beautifully describes the number one priority of modern fencing;
never allow your opponent to use his favorite move, his AoE.

and pay me for private lessons!"); wrong distance ("You were too close"), or stupidity ("Why did you do such a stupid attack?"). As everybody knows from their own experience, these remarks are not at all helpful and do not stop you losing your next match. They only give you a bad conscience ("Why am I so slow again? Why did I let the coach down again?").

Before I start to discuss wins and losses from a new perspective, I would like to mention an anecdote from the New York Fencers Club. My work requires me to travel to the US about four times a year. Whenever possible, I bring my fencing equipment and sometimes have time to fence at the Fencers Club, which is America's oldest and one of its best. Every time has been a unique experience from different points of view. The New York Fencers Club is probably the only fencing club in the world where you pay your floor fee, walk out on the floor, and nobody says hello to you. You just fence. During the three times over the last couple of years that I have been there, nobody has actually bothered to speak to me at all. It is probably the only club in the world where I can be anonymous.

Anonymity has its advantages. Take this scene: a balding fencer in his fifties with short reach (I am only 5 ft. 10 in [1.79 m], which is not much for an epee fencer) walks on to the piste with these top US fencers. It is naturally not difficult to get them into my AoE.

Once I fenced one of the leading women in the country and beat her 15 – 3. After the bout she explained to a friend, "He was no good – he only did sixth disengage." That was her way of describing the defeat. My way is dramatically different. I managed to make her do 15 identical fleche attacks right into my AoE. The traditional way of looking at it is the following: the fencer did 15 stupid attacks. End of story. A traditional coach would therefore probably blame stupidity. Her explanation was that I only did sixth disengage ripostes, which in her world would not be sufficient to parry her normally very good fleche attacks (this assumption was, however, proved wrong). If we assume that my opponent is not stupid (very few fencers are), we should focus on the following question: *How did I get her to do 15 fleche attacks into my AoE?*

This straightforward question is actually nothing less than a change of paradigm. *Do not focus on what you have done well or poorly; focus on your opponent.* There are always two fencers in a bout. Behind all scoring actions from a fencer, there is always a certain set of prerequisites from the opponent that made the scoring action possible. Most of the time, these prerequisites are not obvious. These are what we can call the "hidden prerequisites (HP)."

I sometimes receive invitations to lecture on fencing. To get the audience to understand more clearly the concept of "hidden prerequisites," I sometimes ask them to observe the following situation: a couple is dancing the tango, when suddenly the man steps heavily on the lady's foot. Whose fault is it? In most cases, the audience correctly answers, it is the man (the exception being the Harvard fencing team 2004!). Yet even though the fault is clearly the man's (and it is of no interest whether he did it on purpose or not), there is an HP in this situation: the lady actually had her foot in a position where the man could step on it.

Let's take the following action and analyze it for HP's: fencer A binds fencer B's blade in sixth and scores. Fencer A's HP's could then be: fencer B had to have his arm a bit too extended in his *en garde* position (the elbow should be at around a 90° angle, according to my philosophy), and he had to have his blade pointing towards Fencer A's target area (it should be pointed away from the target in the *en garde* position to decrease the opportunity for binding) and Fencer B had to be too close. These observations have three things in common: they focus on the opponent, they focus on avoiding being hit; and from Fencer B's point of view, they are easily amendable. That is, it should not be difficult for Fencer B to take away Fencer A's HP's.

There are a number of take-home messages from this scenario when assessing wins or losses in fencing bouts. Every hit received is a learning experience. *It is therefore much more interesting to analyze losses than wins.* Fencing is one of the few sports where losers eventually turn into winners. My own career is a prime example of this mechanism. Although I was not even close to getting into the junior epee national team in a small country in northern Europe, this did not stop me from dominating the senior world fencing scene in epee.

Only four fencers have ever succeeded in winning the men's epee individual junior World Championship and also the senior title. Bruno Khabarov (USSR) and Roland Losert (AUT) even managed to win it the same year (1959 and 1963, respectively). Pavel Kolobkov (USSR and Russia) is in a class of his own, winning the junior championship in 1987 and 1988 and the senior title in 1993, 1994, 2000, 2002 and then again in 2005. Fabrice Jeannet (FRA) won the junior in 2000 and the senior in 2003.

The way to analyze your losses and turn them into learning experiences and later victories includes the following steps:

1. *Focus on your opponent.*
2. *Focus primarily on avoiding being hit rather than scoring.*
3. *Find the hidden prerequisites in your fencing that allow your opponent to score.*
4. *Take away these hidden prerequisites.* This can often be done through minor changes in your guard position or fencing distance. Your opponent will then try to hit you in some other way. This will hopefully alter his fencing out of his AoE and closer to your own AoE.

Note that all the changes instituted following point 4 will shift the fencing towards the "more physically-based/less technique-based tactics" endpoint.

It is appropriate to consider fencing bouts as being on a continuous sliding scale between technique-based and physically-based tactics. The endpoints of this scale are maximum technique-based tactics coinciding with minimum physical-based tactics with the primary intention of scoring hits, and maximum physically-based tactics coinciding with minimum technique-based tactics with the primary intention of avoiding being hit. Because of the major shift in world-class epee fencing over the last two decades, it is appropriate to call this sliding scale between the two described endpoints the new fencing dimension. This is especially valid because the analysis of a bout lost will more or less automatically shift the fencing towards the physically-based tactics endpoint (to avoid getting hit).

Most of the time my analysis of a bout lost by one of my students includes the following ingredients: "If your opponent's AoE is XXX, the hidden prerequisites that facilitate his AoE (facilitating HP's) are YYY. Therefore, refrain from YYY and close the distance to limit his choices."[1]

This new fencing dimension gives us the intellectual tool to understand the outcome of fencing bouts and also recommends remedies for losses.[2]

In order to succeed within the new fencing dimension, a fencer needs to master some tactics. Fencers who want to explore these topics in depth right away should turn to the following topics in Chapter 6:

6.1. STEERING (Guiding or forcing your opponent into your own AoE without giving him the blade.)

6.2. DESTRUCTIVE PARRIES (Limiting your opponent's choices to force him into your AoE.)

6.3. CONFUSING PARRIES (Forestalling your opponent's disengagement.)

6.4. CONTROLLING THE DISTANCE (Usually, closing it – Depriving your opponent of the time or space needed for complex phrases.

6.5. BOUNCING: (Solving the "change of direction" vulnerability by landing on both feet with a forward, backward, or in-place jump.)

---

[1] For HP's, facilitating HP's, etc., see Terminology and Chapter 6.

[2] But it also destroyed classical epee fencing and turned the weapon into a rather uninteresting spectator sport. I do not think that any of us that were involved back in 1973 could have understood the consequences of our intellectual efforts.

5.

Developing the New Dimension

This book has so far described the background to my personal journey into advanced fencing strategy. The results of my journey have been described in a number of sequential chapters to maximize the understanding of the rather novel and complex thinking represented by the new fencing paradigm. The reader may falsely assume that the development of the new paradigm was a straightforward exercise. Nothing could be further from the truth. It is worth repeating that I would never have volunteered to spearhead this journey into the unknown initiated by Eric Sollee at MIT if I had not at that point given up any personal fencing ambitions.

The first four years of development (1973 – 1976) were full of confusion; and the outside world, especially within the Swedish fencing establishment, argued that it was a dead-end road. We tried various approaches and often did not know whether we were making progress or were going in the wrong direction.

In the present chapter I would like to discuss the development from a chronological perspective, emphasizing those episodes that caused me to understand that the new paradigm had some viability after all. It is interesting how an unsuccessful junior epeeist who had given up all fencing ambitions could reach the top of world class epee after one year of foil at a NCAA third division fencing university in the US.

Fencing in the US at that time was relatively weak, and surprisingly naive on the international level. For example, the Americans often did not realize when they were being cheated in international competition, and they had no idea what to do about it.

5.1 1975 – 1976: The Army

After my first year at MIT, I was drafted into the Swedish army and served 10 months (1974 – 1975). The service was rather tough. I remember a standard pack – 36 kilos, or just under 80 pounds. It weighed a ton at the beginning and felt like nothing at the end. The Army only let us fence twice a week, but we trained our muscles every day in other ways. I think that year gave me a physiological and psychological robustness that I benefited from for the rest of my fencing career. This was also the period when I started discussing the ideas behind the new paradigm with Björne Väggö. Björne will have more to say later about his own individual development of our ideas (Chapter 7).

As noted earlier, the foundation of the new paradigm had been defined (but not proved) during my year at MIT.

I had entered MIT with the aim of becoming an electrical engineer with a special focus on computers. I had the privilege at MIT to work with the most powerful computers in the world at the time. I remember that I regarded even these computers as "stupid" and I saw no major future for them (!) because I could not anticipate the tremendous development in the electronics area. However, the studies at MIT were a lot of fun. For the first time in my life I could select the courses that I really wanted. The speed of teaching was high enough to keep my full attention, and I could really excel. I naturally took a lot of mathematics and physics courses, but also chemistry, astronomy, programming and others.

I returned to Stockholm after one year at MIT for three different reasons: I was drafted into the Army, I saw no major future for computers, and I wanted to develop my fencing to a higher level than was possible at a US college.

I hoped to continue my studies at the Royal Institute of Technology in Stockholm. The people at the Royal Institute, however, rudely told me that they could not register me as a transfer student. I had to start my studies all over again because "We have no idea what an education at MIT is worth." The result was that after my Army service, I started at the Medical University in Stockholm (Karolinska Institute) with the aim of becoming a physician. Medical studies in Sweden consist of a 7.5 years program and you are expected to enter the program directly from high school without any college preparation. I entertained myself in the army by taking the first year mathematics exams (and some second year exams) at the University of Stockholm in order to transfer credits to my own country. I tried to do the same with the Royal Institute of Technology, but there were a lot of labs where I had to be present in person, so that I couldn't get many credits there.

The teaching tradition in Sweden is rather slow so, in order to make my time at Karolinska Institute a bit more interesting, I started to take courses in economics as well as medicine. As I describe later on, I got fed up both with fencing and with my studies in 1978 and decided to return to MIT again for one term, but this time to study biochemistry, immunology, tumor biology and virology. Again, MIT was a lot of fun. I really liked the speed at which US universities worked. After my return to Sweden in January 1979, I trained full-time for the 1980 Olympics. After I stopped competing at an international level in 1980, I took my PhD 1982, Assoc. Professor (Docent) 1986 and MD 1989.

5.2 1975 – 1977: The Czarnecki Years

While still serving in the Swedish Army, I met a new coach at my club in 1975, Kaj Czarnecki. He was a former epee fencer with top international experience. He also had an open view on how fencing could be done. He immediately understood that the natural consequence of the new paradigm would be that I ran the risk of ending up in close combat situations (infighting) when my timing was slightly off. The timing window in which I decide to make my sixth parry – bind counterattack is narrow and when my timing is slightly off the likely result is that no hit is scored because my opponent manages to block my attempt with his guard. He also has no chance of scoring since his blade is safely bound with my sixth parry – bind. A close combat situation should be advantageous for the shorter and better-prepared fencer. The taller fencer cannot use his greater reach in this situation. Kaj Czarnecki was 1.95 m tall (just over six foot four) and very strong. In addition, he had metal plates underneath his thick leather fencing master's outfit. As a result, Kaj was willing to let me train in close combat with him, an exercise that often left one or both of us bruised or bleeding. In addition to the often exhausting muscular training in the Swedish army, I felt that my abilities increased every day, even if I could train only a couple of times a week.

The rules in the army were strict. We only got leave of absence for World Cup events, so our competitions were limited. There were three of us in the same regiment who would in time have international fencing careers: myself, Björne Väggö and Göran Malkar. Unlike me, Göran was regarded as a fencer with potential. The Swedish Fencing Federation sent him to a World Cup competition in Paris early in 1975, where to his own surprise he won a silver medal. This result made those of us who trained with him realize that we might make it as well. So in the spring of 1975, I decided to enter the number one epee tournament of the year: Heidenheim, in southern Germany.

5.3 1975: Heidenheim

I received no support and traveled to southern Germany on the night train (a distance of nearly 1600 kilometers or 1,000 miles), using my own money. The journey took 24 hours or so.

Heidenheim was combined with the European Cup team event and was the most difficult epee competition in the world to win. The field was far deeper than the Olympic Games or World Championship, since only the best three from each country were allowed into the Olympics and only five in the World Championship at the time. In Heidenheim you need to beat 25 Russians and some 75 Germans among a total of 300 top fencers. In contrast, only 50 fencers enter the Olympics and about 100 take part in the World Championship, many of whom represent countries without top international ambitions. Heidenheim has always been a cutthroat competition. In 1975, there were two preliminary rounds of pools with seven fencers, of whom just three were promoted to the next round, followed by direct elimination (DE) bouts without repechage from 64 fencers to a final of four. The DE from 64 was fenced to 10 hits.

I do not have any specific memories of the preliminary rounds, except that I was very surprised to make it into the last 64. (Because this book is primarily concerned with Olympic touches, bouts before the DE and the finals are of less importance.) In my first direct elimination match I was lucky to get a short, young and very nervous Czech. I felt no sense of triumph after this victory since my opponent practically beat himself, and I only had to hold on to my epee to win. The next match was a completely different story because my opponent was Patrick Picot, a world-class Frenchman who would become Olympic champion in the 1980 team event. I was very nervous to begin with and forgot all about my new paradigm – after all, it was only halfway developed at this time. Due to my nervousness and lack of confidence in the new paradigm, I started to fence in the old classical way.

Picot actually presented all the hidden prerequisites that I needed. He had a nice classical guard with a half extended arm and no bouncing, even though he was rather fast. He was not much taller than me.

Still, he was leading 9 – 6 by the time I started to think. At that point, his teammates packed his things together and shouted rudely to him to finish me off. They also made some very disrespectful remarks about me that are not fit to write in this book. This was the turning point in the match. I shortened the distance, opened my sixth side and waited for his attack. I did not have to wait long and was able to rapidly win the bout with my favorite sixth parry – bind riposte, after which I turned to the French spectators to have them acknowledge my win.

In the next match things got worse as I had to meet the same French crowd that I had angered in the previous match (this time also including Picot) and faced a much better French fencer, Jacques Brodin. He had won a silver medal at the World Championship the previous year, had explosive footwork, and held his French handle far out to extend his reach. His favorite move was a very fast advance-lunge ending on the foot. He never missed that attack. Since he never gave the blade, I did not have the principal and one of the facilitating prerequisites.[1] I only had the non-bouncing prerequisite. Since I had not fenced him before, I again started in classical style with the result that he hit me at will with his lightning attacks to foot. He never missed once, and the French crowd was cheering him on.

Since I had made the last 16, my team management started to observe me. They screamed, "Keep your distance." With Brodin five touches ahead, my thought processes began to kick in. Suppose I *shortened* the distance? If he continued with his foot attacks; wouldn't it be possible to hit him before he extended his arm and gained speed in his attack? So I did exactly the opposite of what my team management advised and to everybody's surprise it worked beautifully. Jacques was in shock and the French crowd was silent. Short distance had worked again (this time combined with a counterattack).

The next bout was against Boris Lukomski, who had won a bronze medal in the previous year's World Championships and would go on to take the silver medal later that year. As I have mentioned, Boris later gave me the final push to write this book.[2]

Before I describe this bout, I should mention that Soviet epee fencing was believed to be virtually unbeatable at the time. The only threat to their dominance came from the communist satellite states, and the majority of the finalists in the World Championships came from Eastern bloc countries. These were the days when doping was not allowed, but testing procedures were inefficient. It was later shown that doping was widespread within communist sports establishments and many athletes used doping under the supervision of physicians. We do not have proof that fencers were among them, but it is reasonable to suspect that at least some were. An additional advantage was that Soviet fencers could expect help from Eastern European referees. Sometimes this help was covert, sometimes not.

---

[1] Again, see Terminology (at the front of this book) and Chapter 6.
[2] Boris is now coaching in Chicago.

More legitimately, they also introduced the new epee strategy: the sixth – second play leading to parry – bind, or beat parry in sixth or second with fleche or advance – lunge attacks. (I will discuss this in more detail in section 6.1.) They were big, fast, very strong and often left-handed. Their new strategy was introduced during the late 60's with Nikantchikov as the big name (World Champion in 1966, 67 and 70 and silver medalist in 1969). When he toured Sweden in 1968 or 69, I was too young to fence him, but I was shocked to see his simple style.

Much later at MIT, I discussed this experience with Eric Sollee. The new paradigm was especially designed to cope with the Soviet strategy. Their style had both my principal HP's and one of our facilitating HP's (non-bouncing), and there were opportunities to provoke the second facilitating HP (half extended arm). (These concepts will be developed in Section 6.6.)

The key was to block all the HP's the Soviets needed. Since they always performed actions with two moves, one of which was blade contact, I needed to avoid all forms of blade contact. And since most of the time they performed their attacks as advance-lunges or fleches, it was also crucial for me to keep a distance that was too short for either action. Since my AoE was (and is) sixth parry – bind, it was also important to get them to go high.

This time I started the bout using half the new strategy. I avoided blade contact but I stood at a classical distance. When Boris picked up speed in his attack, I reacted in such a way that he made blade contact and soon led by four hits. At that point, I was again ordered by my team management to keep my distance, which I fortunately ignored and did the opposite. I closed the distance while making sure that no attacks could land low. I soon found that Boris was unable to cope with this strategy and I could provoke him to half extend his weapon arm, whereupon I had all three of the needed prerequisites and could then hit him at will.

By coming from four touches down against Boris Lukomski, I had made the final four of the most difficult World Cup competition in the world.

Some of my teammates had been so sure that I would lose that they did not even bother to watch. Management congratulated me on reaching the final but also reprimanded me for not following orders.

The final was a different story, unfortunately, since the German Gert Opgenorth broke his blade on my weapon arm and then pushed the whole blade through the arm, nearly to the guard, destroying the main vein. Then he said, "Der Degen gehört mir" (The epee belongs to me!) and pulled it out. Then it really started to bleed!

This was in the middle of my first World Cup final so both my blood pressure and my pulse were sky high and so my arm was spouting blood. Fortunately, the organizers had nurses, surgeons and ambulances present at the competition, which saved my life. The representatives of the Swedish Fencing Federation stayed just long enough to give me my passport the next morning. Then I was alone in a foreign country with the extent of the nerve damage to my arm unknown. Gert Opgenorth sent a postcard and hoped I would survive.

I had to stay in hospital for a week, after which I was transferred to Sweden by ambulance and special air flight, and I recovered rapidly. Some people asked me how I could continue to fence when the fencing outfit at the time was clearly not safe enough and accidents did happen.[1] The answer was that I had no alternative: my urge to prove my point was too strong.

The lessons learned from my first World Cup competition were clear. Short distance, together with the new paradigm, effectively neutralized much better fencers. The new paradigm without short distance did not work for me, only the combination. I could shorten the distance at will and my opponents could do nothing about it; if they increased the distance by retreating, I would immediately shorten the distance again and they would rapidly reach the end of the piste. Some of the best epeeists in the world, including the 1974 and 1975 silver medalists and a

---

[1] Modern fencing equipment is made of ballistic material that precludes this type of accident.

future Olympic team champion, had tried desperately to increase the distance against me but all of them failed. In my mind, this definitely proved the second of the Sollee conjectures: the fencer with the shorter distance *does* decide the fencing distance in a bout. I also thought that my experience in that competition supported (but did not prove) the first of the Sollee conjectures: is it possible for the fencer with the lower technical fencing ability to decide the technical level of the bout? It seemed so. My removal of all my opponent's hidden prerequisites effectively blocked their more technical AoE.

But could they develop a more technically advanced counter move? This conjecture could not be proved at the time because nobody would bother developing technical countermoves against an underdog like me.

At this point I felt that Sollee conjecture No. 2 was proved, but No. 1 and No. 3 might depend on my underdog position and my advantage might disappear once people started to develop countermoves. I took the firm decision to always fence at a short distance and never again at a classical fencing distance. The arm injury, however, was a substantial setback. Fortunately, it healed completely.

5.4 1976: An Olympic Year, But...

The Swedish national team won the epee team competition in the World Championship during the summer of 1975 with the Germans in second place. During that winter, the Germans invited a number of the best teams to their fencing center in Tauberbischofsheim. My federation suspected that they wanted to study the Swedish fencers in order to beat them at the 1976 Olympics and so sent a team that would not participate in the Games. It was there that for the first time I got to fence the reigning World Champion, Alexander Pusch (he also won the 1976 Olympic title and the 1978 World Championship – in total 13 world and Olympic medals). When a TV crew turned up to film Alex for the evening news, by accident they happened to film him against me, expecting an exemplary win. I used the new paradigm from the start and beat him 5 – 0. He had to spend half an hour explaining to the TV viewers what had happened.

Early in 1976, I went to a World Cup competition about which I do not remember much, except that I saw a short and rather slow fencer win bout after bout. He forced his opponent's blade around and around with destructive fourth parries and drew them into his sixth parry – bind riposte. He scored many hits in this identical way against much better opponents. As mentioned, this was exactly what we had proposed during the intellectual exercises at MIT. The fencer was Hungarian, and his name was Jenö Pap.

The difference between the way Pap fenced and what we had imagined was simply this: Pap based his whole strategy on one movement and one movement only. This was another independent support for Sollee conjuncture No. 3: is it possible to force your opponent into your own AoE? I did it now and then, but Pap did it all the time. I was becoming more and more convinced that Sollee conjecture No. 3 was indeed correct, and after the winter of 1975 – 76 I acted as if it were true. I also incorporated Pap's movement into my arsenal and this move would rapidly become my favorite. (Jenö Pap would win the World Championship in 1982.)

Looking back, I realize that I did not prioritize fencing enough during the 1975 – 76 academic year. As previously mentioned, I had added a full-time economics course to my medical school studies. I also underestimated the need for training. The net result was that my international standing did not improve, and at the end of the year I was ranked fourth in Sweden. Normally this ranking would not have been a problem, since the 1976 Olympic team would consist of five fencers plus one reserve.

But for unknown reasons, the Swedish Federation did not select me.

I was stunned. During the Games, I listened to the radio, and when I heard that the Swedish team had won the Olympics I ran a 15-mile race to punish myself. During that run, and after it, I swore over and over again to beat *them*. I had a new motivation for reaching the top: I would show them.

5.5 1977: From Bern to Buenos Aires and Beyond

After the 1976 Games, I arranged my life so that fencing was my number one priority, training up to 20 hours a week. At the same time I accepted all the Sollee conjectures and adjusted my strategy accordingly. The new paradigm was at last completed and ready to launch.

Success was not long in coming. At the 1977 Bern World Cup competition, I had an extremely difficult path to the final: Jürgen Hehn, followed by Alexander Pusch and finally Reinhold Behr, all of them German. Pusch and Hehn had come first and second in the Olympics and Behr was a member of the German team. This was the first full try out for the new paradigm and it was not even exciting. I do not think any of them got more than 6 hits (out of 10) on me. I won the final easily, giving me my first World Cup victory. It was raining heavily that evening in Bern and I just walked for hours in the downpour, feeling as I had never felt before. I felt victory for the paradigm that worked, pride for the thinking initiated at MIT and happiness for Eric Sollee and my other important teachers: my first coach – Meckel – and Czarnecki).

At the end of that season, I was ranked number one in the country and space was found for me in the national team that would participate in the 1977 World Championship in Buenos Aires. I was 21 years old and ready.

The World Championship had 3 preliminary rounds with approximately 6 fencer in each group of which 3 or 4 qualified to the next round: direct elimination from 16 fencers with repechage to a final of 6. I had some problems in one of the preliminary rounds, but otherwise progressed without difficulty through the direct elimination to the final pool of six. I then promptly lost my first two bouts, the first to Rolf Edling and the second to a Swiss (Patrick Gaille) who gave me all the hidden prerequisites I needed so that I thought that I would beat him easily.

After that bout, I sat down to reconsider and my analysis resulted in the following thoughts. I had psychologically prepared for each of the two bouts the same way as for my DE fights. The aim of this preparation was nervous system arousal in order to make sure that I would be "hot". Perhaps that made me too hot in the final, so that I lost the cool calculation needed for success. Fencing is, after all, a balance between opposites. (Examples include: be hot but not too hot, cold but not too cold, fast but not too fast, flexible but not too flexible, strong but not too strong.) I concluded that my psychological preparation before the bouts, together with the enormous pressure from the milieu around the piste (it was a final on a raised piste with nothing else going on in the arena), had made me too hot.

My second thought was that, *if I had this problem, others might have it too.*

Before my third bout, I decided not to make any particular psychological preparations, assuming that the pressure on the piste would make me hot enough. I also decided to be less eager than normal so as to let my opponent have both the opportunity and the time to do something really stupid (as I had done in the first two bouts). This worked beautifully and I won the three remaining bouts. My opponents defeated themselves and made a variety of ill-advised attacks. I had only to hold on to the blade to win. I felt a little sorry for the Swiss Daniel Giger, who had the last bout against me. He studied the scoreboard intensely before the bout and realized he only had to beat me to win the gold medal. Giger used a French grip in such fashion that it withheld some of the hidden prerequisites that I needed. On the other hand, it was written on his face with some desperation that he just had to win this bout. I thought to myself that he would be too hot.

Between hits, Giger took off his mask and let me see his face. I will never forget the combination of pain and desperation. After I had beaten him, four of us had qualified for a barrage: I and my teammate Rolf Edling from Sweden, and Patrick Gaille and Daniel Giger from Switzerland.

I started with Rolf using the tactics I had decided on. Rolf had very strong nerves and normally his face has an energetic expression. In the middle of the bout he removed his mask and to my great surprise his face expressed sorrow. That told me that he was at last ready to commit to something stupid. I just had to wait for my win. After beating Gaille in my second bout, only Daniel Giger was left. The actions of our first bout repeated themselves and I still feel sorry for twice stopping Daniel becoming World Champion.

But I was World Champion myself.

Johan Harmenberg tops the podium as 1977 World Champion. Left: France's Patrice Gaille. Right: Johan's teammate Rolf Edling.

From my perspective, there were several lessons to be learned from this World Championship

The first and most important was that all the fencers were nervous and behaved nervously. That included me for the first two bouts of the final. We all made poor decisions and sometimes did outright stupid attacks that had little chance of success – errors that we would never have made earlier in the competition or even in practice. All the coaches were calling for their students' blood. In my experience, everybody is nervous in a World Championship final, whether they admit it or not. Since I am always nervous (which partly explains my lack of success during my junior years), I am used to the feeling and can handle it, whereas fencers who never experienced the feeling until they reach the final of a World Championship may find it more difficult to act rationally under the influence of nervousness.

The second lesson was that the problems I had over the season to survive preliminary rounds could be due to a combination of two factors.

1) I am always nervous. Other fencers are not. This means that I am more liable to make mistakes by being too hot in the early rounds. This evens out during the course of the competition if I survive, and it turns into a competitive advantage in the final.

2) Because early bouts are less important than later ones, few hits can be categorized as Olympic touches and my whole paradigm was designed to deal with Olympic touches, which also contributed to my problems.

One result of my possibly unusual temperament was that I was either knocked out early or won. In my career I have very few results between first and sixty-fifth or so. I needed to design a procedure that made sure I won the right competitions. I will discuss this in Chapter 8, which deals with my personal methods.

5.6 A Bitter Year and a Return to MIT: 1977 – 1978

The aftermath of my success in the World Championship was bitter. One of the key elements of my success was that I had been able to train once a week with national team members during the preceding year. My own club did not have any other elite fencers, so this training was critical for me. Immediately after my win, I was forbidden to participate in national team training. No real reason was given other than "lack of space." At the same time the fencing environment around my coach, Kaj Czarnecki, made it impossible for him to develop world-class fencers; he subsequently resigned and took the position of national coach to the US Modern Pentathlon team.

At the time, I had a problem understanding the lack of support from the Swedish fencing establishment. I still have a problem, but I understand it slightly better. It is important to appreciate that Sweden had a world-class epee team even without me and had won the team event at the 1976 Olympics. I seemed to threaten the integrity of that team because I went against all the dogmas that existed at the time.

Everything that I did contradicted the official view. I combined fencing with high-level academic studies and had developed some parts of my fencing in a US academic environment. I had not had any fencing success as a junior. Most importantly, I had a style that was dramatically different from everybody else's, and I trained in another fashion. I might still have been forgiven all these "faults," but on top of them, I fenced for the "wrong" club! (Still, having a World Champion in the team would have been a matter of pride in most countries.)

In the end, the personality of some of the individuals in the Swedish fencing establishment made the clash inevitable. In 1977, this seemed the greatest tragedy of my life. But the focus of this book is on fencing strategy, rather than fencing politics.

At the time, however, my situation was critical – no coach and no world-class training partners. I did not change my training schedule and continued at medical school. The 1977 – 78 season was lost. This was partly due to the factors mentioned above, which are part of my individual history. Another reason is of much more general application: it is one thing to become world-class – particularly a World Champion – and it is a completely different thing to remain at that level. Once you are a world-class fencer, particularly a World Champion, everything changes. You are always expected to win. More importantly, you demand success from yourself: you start to fear losses more than you enjoy victories. Finally, because you now command respect, other fencers start to analyze your style and try to design strategies to exploit your weaknesses.

All these pressures led me to one conclusion: either I would stop fencing altogether, or I would make one last dedicated effort to win the 1980 Olympic epee title. I selected the latter. My approach was to change fencing from being the highest priority in my life to being the only priority in my life, with the objective of winning the Olympics even on a bad day. (It worked – I had a bad day at the Olympics, but I won anyway.) I prepared a 2-year program, during which all activities in my life were channeled towards reaching my goal, including eating, sleeping and dreaming.

First, I needed to return to MIT and my old coach Eric Sollee. I came back for the fall semester of 1978. (At the same time, I took a number of graduate courses.) The feeling of total support from the MIT fencing team was overwhelming and the contrast to Sweden could not have been greater. Eric helped me find my fencing roots again.

And as Geoff Pingree shows in the following section, Eric's fencing laboratory was developing results on its own.

5.7 Geoff Pingree: MIT Moves Forward

While Johan was working on Eric's ideas in Sweden, Eric Sollee continued his program back in the States. The Massachusetts Institute of Technology (MIT) was an unusual place to develop fencers. While the school's fencing team had existed since the end of the 19th century, MIT had always emphasized academic work and not athletics. While many American schools actively recruit athletes, including fencers, for their athletic programs, this was not MIT's policy. In fact, when Eric began coaching at MIT his attempts to recruit fencers were frustrated when the applicants he recruited found they had to spend more time studying and could only practice once a week, an amount Eric felt was insufficient to field a good team. Still, over the next few years, a confluence of events would lead to the rapid development of a powerful fencing program at "Tech."

As Johan has written, three new freshmen arrived at MIT in 1973 – all with fencing experience and eager to develop their game. This was the first bit of good luck for Eric in developing his team. In the spring of 1974, Johan, Arlie Sterling and Rich Reimer won the prestigious Little Iron Man foil team trophy at the Intercollegiate Fencing Association Championship, intercollegiate fencing's oldest tournament and at that time probably still its strongest. This helped to establish MIT as a place where serious fencing could be pursued. As we have seen, Johan, who had started to develop his new paradigm with Eric here in the States, had left MIT to continue developing his game back in Europe. He was to be replaced with the future national champion, Mark Smith, who joined with Arlie and Rich in 1975 to win the Iron Man for a second year.

This was the context I entered in my freshman year in 1976. I was lucky enough to join a team that had a strong record of success and achievement. While it could be said that the team's accomplishment was based on a small group of extraordinarily talented individuals, the success of the next years were to be the result of the ideas set in motion when Johan was at the school and continued to be developed by Eric Sollee.

As I have said, the most competitive collegiate teams in the US recruited their fencers from the best young fencers from at home and abroad. Unfortunately for Eric, MIT did not actively support recruiting, and as a result, Eric had found this was not a successful strategy. While a few experienced fencers did make it to MIT, Eric found it a challenge to field a full competitive team. He started seeking the best athletes from his beginner physical education classes. He made himself available at all hours of the day or night to give lessons, to help accommodate the difficult academic schedule of his students. Eric also made the MIT fencing room a destination for the best fencers in New England; this provided the MIT students with a high level of competitive training without having to travel extensively. Here MIT fencers could learn and be mentored by the most experienced fencers in the area. Thus Eric was able to create a context that enabled him to maintain MIT's high level of fencing achievement.

Johan, Arlie Sterling and Rich Reimer had arrived at MIT just as Eric was taking over the coaching position there. As Johan has written, the three of them met early and none of them had a desire to put their fencing on hold until the "official" fencing season had started. Silvio Vitale, who was then the head coach, was shifting the coaching of the men's team over to Eric while he concentrated on starting a varsity team for the women. Silvio, exasperated by the three freshmen's insistence on starting their training at the beginning of the term, asked Eric to see what he could do to accommodate these pesky freshmen.

These were the conditions under which Eric would meet the team that was eventually to win the Iron Man Trophy. Somehow or other, the three new friends found a way to start their training early. Arlie and Rich were trained in the foil. Eric, seeing the potential depth he had in this weapon, convinced Johan to switch from epee to foil. Oddly enough, in the view of the succeeding history, Johan had felt that his competitive future in fencing was at an end. This made it easy for him to say yes to Eric's request.

This is where Johan found himself at the start of the fencing season, in a new country, in an unusual intellectual environment and pursing a new weapon. He topped this all off by changing his grip from a traditional simple French handle to one of the new orthopedic or "pistol" grips, and, because of this change, stopped using his parry 4 riposte, which he had considered his most potent fencing move. Johan's feeling that he was not going to make a fencing champion, combined with his exposure to a new coach with a very unique background and approach allowed him an opportunity for radically rethinking his fencing game.

Eric's coaching style followed two tracks. While recruiting fencers had not proven fruitful, MIT did get a few students each year with prior fencing experience. Many of these fencers had developed unique fencing styles. Eric felt very strongly that it was his job to analyze the game the fencers had already developed and to work with them to develop it further, rather than redesign their game to conform to some "classical" ideal. He also found that MIT students were not eager to relearn a new fencing game: they were often opinionated and had put considerable thought into their own games. Rather than "retrain" a fencer into a more "correct" method, Eric would offer a penetrating analysis to each fencer, and engage him or her to look critically at his game and take part in his own development.

Mark Smith presents a good example of how Eric treated the more experienced fencers on the team. Mark had a well-developed game before coming to MIT. As a freshman, he had a very strong attack in the low lines. Although this was very effective against his opponents, Eric discussed this with him as a potential weakness. Eric had figured out this move and was able to defeat Mark with a counter action designed to take advantage of Mark's strongest attack. The summer after his freshman year, Mark returned home and worked with his old coach on the issues that Eric had brought up. When he returned the next year Eric could see the improvement and the deeper complexity of Mark's game. This was typical of what Eric expected in a fencer: an active critique and analysis by the fencer, and engagement in the means to develop his own game.

I remember conversations with Mark about this topic, which were very helpful to me. Mark believed that a fencer could not be a passive student, but, as Mark would put, needed to learn "how to win" – that is, a strategy for bouting that went beyond technique, in other words, that technique needed to be put at the service of this greater strategy. As Mark developed his game, he often conferred with Eric, but it was never a situation where Mark would put himself in a passive student-teacher relationship. As Mark was preparing to graduate from MIT, he and Eric conferred on what coaches might be best for Mark to work with to further develop his game. Eric would always encourage his fencers to get lessons with other coaches, to actively critique these coaches' techniques for themselves and figure what lessons could be learned (or not learned) from them. Mark eventually became USA National champion in the foil and one of the most successful fencers to come out of the MIT program.

While Eric worked to develop the games of the experience fencers he did get at MIT, he also needed to recruit and develop athletes who were brand new to the sport. By this time it was very rare for the top American fencing colleges to develop their fencers from scratch – all the top competitors in the collegiate leagues had considerable fencing experience prior to going to university.

Despite this, Eric was to put together a string of success with athletes new to the sport. The paradigm he was developing with Johan was to prove fruitful in the MIT environment.

Fencing clubs are scarce in the US; at that time, they could mostly be found in the major cities. Coming from a small town in New Hampshire, I was lucky to have taken a short introductory course in fencing given by a local enthusiast. I was intrigued by the sport, and when I arrived at MIT in '76 I sought out Coach Sollee, who invited me to try out for the team.

At this time, Johan had left MIT (to return later). The foilist Mark Smith had joined Arlie Sterling and Rich Reimer and together they comprised the core talent on the team. MIT's results had brought some attention to the fencing program, attracting more experienced fencers to apply for admission, as well as motivating MIT athletes proficient in other sports to think of going out for fencing. Several excellent fencers and athletes joined the team: George Gonzalez-Rivas, John Rodriques, Jim Freidah and Eric Debeus are just a few of the people responsible for high results in the following years.

Looking back, I can see many subtle differences to the environment at MIT at that time compared to most other salles d'armes. The standard model was based on the primacy of a master; he was the center of activity of the club. There is a romantic strain in fencing that sought to make the club like a medieval guild or monastery, with the master as the "pope" and the focus for all knowledge. The MIT club, while not immune to these romantic notions, was, under Eric's direction, more like a research laboratory. Eric never claimed to be the sole source of fencing knowledge, but encouraged his fencers to be actively engaged in thinking out solutions for themselves, most of our training had slight but important differences from the classical models. It was this idea of the salle d'armes as a research lab that allowed people like Johan and Mark Smith to thrive at MIT.

Footwork was fundamental to our approach, but while classical footwork emphasized perfect form, we concentrated on speed, strength, tempo and distance. We did hundreds of "suicide" strips

– footwork exercises down the length of the strip at maximum effort – always pushing for speed and endurance, not just form. While a classical model would not accept fencers beginning to bout before they had proven the perfection of their footwork, this was impractical at MIT, where Eric needed to field a team from scratch. So intensive bouting was begun immediately after the fencer had the rudiments of footwork.

Eric had put together a vibrant community around the fencing room, encouraging many experienced fencers to come to the salle, and encouraging them to help train and mentor the MIT students. Many of the best competitors came also, providing valuable bouting experience.

I had started fencing in foil, and was engaged in ferocious competition with the other foilists on the squad, trying to get on the team. Eric decided to move me to epee, a move I first fought against. But, after a week fencing epee I went to a local tournament and took first place. After this, it became difficult for me to complain to Eric about the change.

Arlie Sterling had moved from foil to epee and he was the first epeeist I studied. Arlie was tall and lanky, unlike myself, yet he was in constant motion on the strip, his own variation on Johan's bouncing. I took this up, with Eric's encouragement, and made it a foundation of my game. I worked with Eric, the former boxer, to develop movement, tempo and distance. Soon I was jumping rope and doing speed bag work to develop leg and hand speed and endurance. The actual blade work I did tended to be very simple. I came to the conclusion that the foundation of fencing consisted of controlling the distance and tempo and having the strength and conditioning to push the opponent into a realm where he would be uncomfortable.

This idea was further reinforced to me when Johan returned the next year. Johan had the epeeists do the simplest bladework: simple counter-sixth ripostes with the point of the weapon traveling up the length of the arm. This further reinforced our ideas that bladework cannot "outwit" a control of distance and tempo. Instead we needed to "train" our opponents, using destructive parries and beats, and to confuse them with our superior distance and legwork and by using what Eric referred to as "absence of blade" techniques and Johan calls "no blade." This further persuaded us to work on our control of the opponent's distance. Fencers measure their distance largely with their blades, so by training ourselves to be able to maintain the distance without the blade we could confuse our opponents while not losing our own distance.

Perhaps it was easier for Americans, who were less mentally burdened by the ancient traditions of fencing than Europeans, to see the logic of Eric and Johan's approach – our model for combat was more likely to be Muhammad Ali than Aldo Nadi – and Ali's phrase, "Float like a butterfly, sting like a bee" aptly summarized our aspirations as fencers.

When Johan returned to MIT in the fall of 1978, he found me bouncing like Ali (and like Johan himself!), and using absence of blade and destructive parries. While we had not yet developed the paradigm with the clarity that Johan gives it here, we were definitely onto something, as the results showed. I won the IFA epee championship and with John Rodriquez and Robert Schoenberger, took the IFA team epee championship. Not one of us had any substantive fencing experience before coming to MIT. George Gonzalez-Rivas, our sabre man, also learned all his fencing at MIT, and was named All-American. With Eric Debeus, our foilist, we tied for second place at the NCAA championships, finally receiving 3rd place on indicators. This was the best showing for MIT in its history – and showed a depth of talent that was unusual for a school that did not actively recruit fencers.

As I talked with Johan over the years, he always came back to the idea of writing a book on his conclusions on fencing strategy. I was intrigued and encouraged him to do so. While my own fencing was strongly influenced by Johan, we had never developed his ideas to such a refined and rigorous level.

When we put my own experience and that of the MIT fencing team into context with the rest of this book, a number of interesting conclusions can be drawn. The development of Johan's fencing in Europe between 1974 and 1978 had independently been paralleled by the MIT fencing team and had reached a similar developmental level by the fall of 1978 when Johan returned to MIT. Using the vocabulary of this book, we had mastered the critical parts of the new paradigm. No blade, destructive parries, fencing that aimed to steer the opponent into the fencers AoE. A lot of mobility, aiming to steer the fencing into a distance that was awkward for the opponent while providing opportunities for high point speed scoring by rapid arm extension movements.

In addition, Johan's own development had reached a plateau after winning the 1977 World Championship. His experience at the MIT fencing "research lab" now with a similar level of strategic fencing thinking during the fall of 1978, was critical for his continued development and the refinement of the strategy that would win him the Olympic gold medal 1980.

5.8 Johan Continues: 1978 – 1979

Returning to MIT and working with Eric was a lot of fun. We decided that the best way to handle my problem of surviving the preliminary rounds was to make sure that I controlled when I performed at my best by undergoing a one-month rigorous peak enforcement program before the event. (This personal program is laid out in Chapter 8, and I want to emphasize that it is not for everyone.) We also considered that it was not realistic to expect me to reach an enforced peak more than twice yearly. These events, we decided, would be Heidenheim 1979 and 1980 (both in April), the World Championship in July 1979 and the Olympic Games in July 1980.

Our plan meant that I basically gave up all other competitions in order to do well on these four occasions. Not even the Swedish championships were on my list. As discussed in detail below, I managed to win three of these four competitions, the exception being the 1979 World Championship in Australia, where I never managed to master the time difference.

We doubled my training schedule from 10 – 20 hours to 20 – 40 hours a week until the Olympics, with the objective of winning even if I had a bad day. I managed to preserve the quality of training because I was driven by a goal. This was not only to win the Olympics. I also wanted to prove my point to the Swedish fencing establishment. I wanted revenge.

Feeling much stronger, I returned to Sweden at the end of December 1978. From that time until the Olympics fencing would be my only priority in life, undisturbed by work or studies. From January 1979, I gave up studying and fenced full time.

Since all the components of the new paradigm were now in place, all aspects of training and competing were working as planned. I won Heidenheim in the spring of 1979 without much problem. My only memory of a key opponent, Rassolka from the Soviet Union, was the loud and furious quarrel between his three or four coaches about how he should score the next hit against me. "Go high!" "Go low!" "Parry-riposte!" – and so on. Finally they settled for "Straight fleche high." But we had two coaches who understood Russian and they translated for me. This was one of the few occasions when I used my weak fourth parry-riposte.

I firmly believe that it was a weakness of the Soviet system that their fencers had to accept orders from the sidelines.

5.9 The Final Effort: 1979 – 1980

After the 1979 World Championship, all my efforts were concentrated on the Olympics. I felt certain that my main rivals would be practicing counter moves against me. I needed to come up with something new so they would be chasing a moving target. The unorthodox moves that I had pioneered so successfully were now expected by my opponents and were thus no longer a surprise. As Sun-Tzu stated, the unorthodox can turn into the orthodox to form the basis for a new unorthodox/orthodox relationship. He also said that it is only possible to win with the unorthodox.

I decided to introduce a classical fourth parry-riposte into my arsenal, which would complement my fencing, but also be surprising to my opponents. This movement needs a lot of classical fencing talent, which, as previously admitted, I did not have. But

I had been blinded by my own success and truly believed that I could learn to master this move at a world-class level[1]. In retrospect, it was naïve of me to even dream of mastering this difficult move, particularly since the rationale of my developing the new paradigm was that I did not have sufficient classical fencing talent. It is an irony of fate that I failed to perfect this move at a world-class level, yet it won me the Olympic gold medal anyway. More about that later.

In preparation for the Olympics, I took part in around 10 training camps spread over the preceding year. In one of the first camps, Rolf Edling suddenly came onto my piste one morning to fence me. Rolf had won the World Championship in 1973 and 1974 and was still a formidable contender. He was tall and left-handed, he made phenomenally accurate hits to hand, and he had a good mental attitude. He also had a fast extension of his weapon arm. His disadvantage was a lack of mobility, so that he risked very few attacks. I had to use my very fast footwork to wear him down. There were no easy wins against Rolf. Still, I was surprised that he volunteered to fence me because he had to work hard against me, which he did not like, particularly in the morning.

The first thing that happened was that he performed a long advance-lunge with a feint towards my outside high line and a disengage down to my leg. I took a rather defensive sixth parry, which unintentionally let his attack through.

I was stunned. First, Rolf had volunteered to fence me, and then he made an attack! I did not know which of the two was more surprising. Then he did the same thing again. I was still in

---

[1] It may be surprising for the reader that a simple fourth parry-riposte in epee require a lot of talent to execute on an international level, since it is one of the first parries a beginner tries to use. But compared to a fourth parry-riposte, the sixth parry-riposte can be executed with a forward motion and with full control of OP's blade all the way to the touch. Also, the fourth parry-riposte, like any other, can be taken early or late. But an early fourth parry-riposte leaves OP with a range of alternatives: OP can disengage, counter-parry the riposte, or just wait to score with a remise when the riposter has to release the blade. A late executed fourth parry-riposte makes disengage more problematic for the OP (but not impossible), but it adds the risk that OP will score before the late parry has been executed, while the other risks remain largely unaltered.

shock from the surprise of the first attack, and the next one came through as well.

At that point, a thought shot through my head like lightning: He thought he had figured me out!

Rolf was too slow to attack normally, and nobody in the world could make compound attacks against me. It was against all the developments of my paradigm. I could easily shorten the distance and wait for his attack; then I would make my favorite sixth parry – bind riposte in one forward motion as a counterattack. His action would give me all the hidden prerequisites that I needed for my AoE. Great.

But there was no reason to let Rolf know about that just then.

After that, in every training camp, I concentrated on a very difficult task: I had to let through all of Rolf's high – low attacks, but block everything else. It was very difficult, especially since Rolf, who was also cunning, only did that particular attack about once every training camp! However, I managed to let through all those attacks in all training camps and competitions during the 7 months preceding the Olympics.

5.9.1 Heidenheim

The training went well and I was nearly too successful, even in competitions that I did not prioritize. As previously mentioned, Heidenheim was my priority competition before the Olympics. It was more difficult to win this event in 1980 than the year before, because it was apparent that many fencers had done their homework against me. I had to include some unorthodox actions to win my bouts.

In the semifinal against Alexander Pusch, I got a rather easy lead of 8 – 5, but then Alex started fencing in a really superb way. In the early part of the fight he had tried unsuccessfully to increase the distance. At 5 – 8 down he began to decrease the distance – even further than my own comfort zone – but he still refused to attack. This intensive fencing went on for several minutes without anyone scoring.

My nerve broke first. I felt that we were so close that sooner or later he would score and so I had to attack. Wrong. Alex had the best fourth parry-riposte in the world: he took it very late so disengagements were almost impossible, and he used it over and over again. In this way he equalized at 8 – all.

I was in trouble. I needed to do something unorthodox. I knew two things: he would not attack and he would make a fourth parry-riposte if given the opportunity. I did not have the classical fencing talent to time a perfect disengagement. So I came up with a solution. We were both right-handed. Suppose I made a straight fleche attack to his fourth side but *angled towards his rear shoulder* so that my hand was as far away from Alex as possible. He would take his fourth parry, but I would be coming towards him from the far outside (aiming at his rear shoulder and with an angle between blade and arm). If he timed his parry normally (late to discourage disengages), it would arrive too late simply because his hand was naturally held forward and my angled attack would cause his parry to end on the forte of my blade near the guard. I attacked and…

… in actual fact, his parry ended on the base of my thumb. If he had performed a stop thrust, I would have run onto his point, lost the match and felt stupid. Yes, it was unorthodox, but it worked, although for many years I had two scars on my thumb as a souvenir of my 10 – 8 victory.

In the final, I met Aleksandr Abushackmetov, one of the best Soviet fencers. He had also done his homework and I was exhausted after my semifinal. He took an early lead by withdrawing all of the HP's that I needed. I took many destructive fourth parries in the air to get him towards my sixth side, but he refused these invitations.

Then suddenly the situation changed completely. He got orders from his coach to make a feint – disengage attack to my fourth line. He was unhappy with the advice but followed it anyway. After his disengage, his blade ended on my sixth side, right in the middle of my AoE. Then I had all the hidden prerequisites I needed and got an easy win. I had passed another milestone.

5.9.2 The 1980 Olympics

The 1980 Moscow Olympic Games, which I had lived for, finally arrived. If I remember correctly, there were 2 preliminary rounds with groups of 6 fencers with 3 qualifying to next round. There was a direct elimination from 16 fencers with repechage to a final of 6 fencers. After some problems in my first direct elimination match against the Italian Bellone, I ended up in the six-man final.

The final was a very strong pool containing two Swedes, me and Rolf Edling, Philippe Riboud of France, Ernö Kolczonay of Hungary, the Russian Aleksander Mojaev and the Romanian Mihai Popa. This final would be Popa's best result. Mojaev would peak with a silver medal in the 1981 World Championships. Kolczonay was at the beginning of a 10-year run during which he was constantly among the leaders; he had finished second to Riboud in the World Championship the previous year. Rolf, as I have said, had a long and distinguished career: 3rd in the 1971 World Championships, 5th in 1972, World Champion in 1973 and 1974. He was sixth in the 1976 Olympics and second after me in the 1977 World Championship. Then, of course, there was Riboud, who would also be a two-time individual World Champion, and was, as I have said, the most brilliant technical fencer I have ever seen.

In short, it was a very challenging final. There were three tall fencers – Rolf, Mojaev and Popa – three left-handers – Rolf, Riboud and Mojaev – and two fencing with a French grip – Riboud and Kolczonay. The three attributes, tall, left-handed and French grip, all gave me added complications.

I started with Rolf. To my pleasant surprise, he immediately executed the attack that I had secretly encouraged during the last 6 – 7 months. He did not do it once, but four times within the first 30 seconds, with the result that I led 4 – 1 (three single hits and one double). Then he changed to his normal tactics, but I managed to squeeze out another double for a 5 – 2 victory.

After the bout, we had a conversation that became rather famous in Swedish fencing circles. Rolf said, in his characteristic drawl: "You did not fence like that in practice." I replied, using the same drawl: "No, Rolf, I did not fence like that in practice, but now it is a competition, it is the Olympics, it is even the final of the Olympics."

Then I met Riboud. I had planned and rehearsed my tactics against him for months. Since I took it for granted that he had studied me, I felt that I had to introduce something new to beat him. This was the plan: I would start with parry-riposte tactics, while hopefully he would fence anticipating my standard counterattacks. This should keep the bout even to 3 – all or so, after which I would change to my counterattack tactics. With luck, he would not immediately understand that I had changed tactics and I could win the bout.

This plan backfired immediately. Even though I had practiced parry-ripostes for more than a year, my classical talent was not good enough to cope with a fencer of Riboud's class. At 1 – 3 down, I changed tactics to counterattack mode, my standard way of fencing. This time Philippe did not catch on immediately and I managed to equalize at 4-all. At this point we both took off our masks to wipe sweat from our faces and I looked into Philippe's rather expressionless face. I then knew two things: Philippe would expect me to continue my successful standard counterattack tactics and would not dream that I might return to the parry-ripostes that had been so unsuccessful earlier in the bout.

If I returned to the parry-riposte tactics, would he catch on? I looked into his face again and said to myself, no way. After some fencing, I managed to take a parry-riposte and end the bout with a win.

My next bout was against Ernö Kolczonay, who used a French handle and had a fencing style that was very difficult for me. He was one of the few top fencers in the world whom I had never beaten. Amazingly, the Riboud fight repeated itself. I started out with the same parry-riposte tactics, which again failed. As in the previous match, I changed tactics at 1 – 3 down and equalized with counter–attacks. It was again down to the last hit. At this point, Ernö avoided looking into my eyes as we wiped sweat from our faces and, as I had against Philippe, I took it as a sign that

JH vs. Popa: the last single hit in JH's last win in the 1980 Olympics. JH has maneuvered Popa so most of his body weight is on his front foot as he tries to bind JH's non-existent blade with Popa's AoE in second. Popa is now trying to retreat but it is a bit difficult for him. JH extends his arm with an advance and hits. Relative speed is 3+, so Popa cannot parry or retreat. JH's high guard is intended to block any high stop thrusts (not needed here).

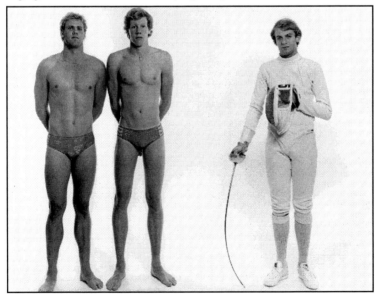

Sweden, population 8,000,000 produced 3 Gold Medallists in the 1980 Olympics. From Left, Pär Arvidsson – Men's 100 meter Butterfly. Bengt Baron – Men's 100 meter Backstroke, JH.

JH with his Gold Medal, 1980 Olympic Games:
"My whole body suddenly felt light…I felt an enormous release of

Ernö would not expect me to change back to parry-riposte tactics. It was a great satisfaction to beat him for the first time with a parry-riposte.

Next up was Popa and since he was a classical fencer I used my standard game throughout the bout to win.

In my last bout I faced Mojaev, who did not have any victories. But at this point my nerve broke completely. I had only one thought in my head: if I win, I will be Olympic champion. Naturally, I lost. But it did not matter, since the others defeated each other and I won the title anyway.

The Olympic Games were a natural point at which to end the high-level competitive part of my life and to move on to other interests.

5.10 After the Olympics: Personal Questions

People often ask me "How does it feel to win Olympic gold?" and "Was it worth the effort?" They generally expect me to answer "fantastic" to the first and "yes" to the second, and often I do as an easy way out. The reality is much more complex and I always feel dishonest when I take the easy way out. I will therefore use a couple of pages of this book to develop my thinking a bit.

5.10.1 How does it feel to win Olympic gold?

The last bout of the 1980 Olympics was between Ernö Kolczonay and Rolf Edling. If Edling won, there would be a barrage between him and me. If he lost but scored more than one hit, he would take silver. If he lost 5 − 1 or 5 − 0, he would come fourth. I had difficulty watching the bout: I didn't want a barrage! I found a loudspeaker in the dressing room that was connected to the referee's microphone and when I heard him say "gauche" (left) five times, I knew that I was the Olympic champion. The feeling was fantastic. I ran back to the stadium as fast as I could to meet the cheering crowd. The ceremony was performed immediately afterwards and I remember, when I heard my name called, my whole body suddenly felt extremely light and I flew up on the podium. I felt an enormous release of the pressure that had built up before the Olympics, my own expectations and those of others. It was like a giant had pushed down on my shoulders for the two long years of my personal Olympic campaign. The target was winning the Olympics even if I had a bad day. I had a bad day, but I won anyway. All that pressure was suddenly released and I flew to the podium. The feeling of happiness was replaced with mere relief.

But while on the podium, I felt nothing, no happiness, nothing. A question made its uninvited appearance: "What do I do now?" Some people seem so happy when they win that they try to capture the moment for as long as possible. I just wanted to go home. I slept more or less continuously for a month before I started to resemble something like a human being again. Suddenly, I felt tired and old.

I returned to medical school, but everything was grey. It felt as if life did not have a purpose anymore. Compared with my Olympic campaign, going to medical school was no challenge. There were no winners and no losers. There was no challenge. I realized that concentrating on the Olympics the way I had was the ultimate ego trip. For two years I had only thought about myself. Me, me, me. Compared with this, most other things in life were naturally colorless. I had devoted myself to it 100%. I trained, ate, slept and rested, but everything was focused on winning the Olympics. It had been my only purpose in life. I was obsessed.

Most areas of life involve compromises. It is not normal to concentrate 100% on something for so long. After the Olympics, I fell, out of control, for a year without finding the ground, without any goal or purpose. In retrospect, I understand that I was experiencing a depression that took me nearly a year to resolve. I did not have any problem passing my medical exams and, in my spare time, I did the final experiments for my Ph.D. Outside observers would probably have seen this as very meaningful. But for me, compared with the feeling of my Olympic campaign, it was so undemanding.

During this period my body longed to train hard again, but I understood that doing this would have been the road to unhappiness. What would have been the purpose? To win the Olympics again? Why? I had nothing left to prove. I was 26. Continuing high-level fencing could easily have turned me into a disillusioned 36-year-old looking back on a life of endless summers in training camps. It would certainly have made me feel like a loser in the end, even if I had won more gold medals. I am happy that, even though I had a depression and my body longed for hard training, I was determined enough to wind fencing down. I am now convinced that if I had continued high-level fencing, I would never have been able to answer "yes" to the question: "Was it worth it?"

During the post-Olympic year, in the middle of 1981, I fell in love with my future wife, Ulrika. I had a purpose in life again. I continued competing on a national level until my son was born in 1987. I never stopped fencing completely, but just continued recreationally. I had successfully made the adjustment to a "normal" life. But the price I paid had been high. Even though I know that I actually did it, and did it all by myself, winning the gold medal, it does not feel real. It is more like it was another person winning, a hypothetical twin. It is not normal to totally devote one's life as I did, and I still have problems emotionally understanding that I was that abnormal devotee.

5.10.2 A Fable

Let me sum it up in a little story:

You are a child running down a road with lots of friends. It is not a race, it is just for fun. It is easy running and you do not get tired. It is pleasant, sunny weather, and you run together with your best friends. Further down the road is a door that is closed but seems to be interesting. What can be behind it? The gang of youngsters reach the door, open it without effort and find a new road, so they keep running. You pass door after door and behind each one you find a new road.

After a while, you are still running, but you are not a child anymore, so you look around. There are fewer people now running with you. They do not look that friendly anymore. The road is narrower and the running is not that easy or pleasant. You look for the next door, a big one. Maybe there is an interesting answer behind it. But leading to it is a narrow path leading to a secret door at the top of a hill. That must hide something really worth knowing. You open it – only to look out at a golden door on top of a mountain.

This time, there is no path and the terrain is totally uncharted. Deep inside your heart, you sense that this is the last and final door and behind it you will find happiness and the meaning of life. You start running up the mountain. The weather is cold and the wind is against you. You are all alone as you fight your way to the last and final door. You open it and jump through and find… nothing. You keep falling without ever reaching the ground.

5.10.3 Was it worth it?

The short answer is yes, maybe. I was in the happy position that I could still develop my life outside fencing. Partly, this was because I was not a child fencing star. I grew up in an environment in which the ruling dogma was that fencing should not be combined with challenging studies. I gave up a computer engineering education at MIT and studied medicine instead, which was my second choice, but others are forced to give up so much more than I had to.

On the other hand, I do not think that I had a completely free choice. I was driven forward by a power stronger than life. I wanted to show the world that my strategy worked and to show the Swedish fencing establishment that I could win. I was also tired of doing things at 50% capacity, like most people. I wanted to know what my ultimate limit was.

The really big reward was not actually winning the gold medal, although that was very nice. No, it was that for the first and only time in my life I was able to do something to 100% of my ability, to find my own limits. To be able to say to myself that there was nothing, absolutely nothing that I could have done to prepare myself better. The road was much more important than the goal.

I think I would have been equally satisfied with my fencing career if I had not won the gold medal. I would have still done my very best. I could not have done more.

It was the ultimate ego trip, but I suffered loneliness before the Olympics and meaninglessness after. The fun of fencing disappeared during this period.

On balance, I would say even in retrospect that the effort was worthwhile – but only just. I am happy that my children seem to be so much more mature about fencing. Both of them fence for fun. Competitively, but for fun.

6.

Technique and Strategy

6.1 Steering Your Opponent Into Your AoE

The hallmark of the new fencing paradigm is to limit the choices of your opponent and to steer him into your AoE. This can be accomplished by destructive parries, confusing parries, and control of the distance.

6.1 Destructive Parries:

Essential to the new physically-based tactics is the ability to steer your opponent without giving him the blade. It is of primary importance to limit his choices and thereby increase the predictability of the action. We explored this area in the 70's by using a number of movements that we now call "destructive parries."

The concept of destructive parries was a natural evolution of the new fencing dimension, but it was not developed during the 1973 – 74 season, even though the possibility was discussed. It was developed shortly afterward by me in Sweden and independently by the MIT fencing team. When I returned to MIT in 1978, all of the best fencers at MIT used this concept. (The evolution at MIT is described by Geoff Pingree in a separate chapter.)

The term "destructive *parry*" is not totally appropriate since the objective of the parry is not to parry your opponent's blade but rather to limit his aggressive possibilities and steer him into your own AoE. The movements of destructive parries do superficially resemble the textbook parries that we can call constructive parries. But the movements of destructive parries are performed more or less regardless of the blade movement of your opponent. The primary objective of a constructive parry is to establish blade contact so as to deflect the opponent's blade. This may be achieved regardless of whether blade contact has been established.

I did not invent my favorite destructive parry. I saw the Hungarian fencer Jenö Pap (1982 World Champion) in one of the later stages of a World Cup competition in 1975 or 1976. He was neither tall nor fast, so why was he still in the competition? The reason was that he crept closer and closer to his opponent while enveloping the blade with his fourth destructive parry. (This was in the days when fencers still extended the arm and the blade.) When his opponent tried to attack with a disengage out of Pap's repeated fourth destructive parries, he often eventually ended on Pap's sixth side. At this point Pap did his favorite sixth parry – bind riposte and scored.

As mentioned previously, this movement suited my new fencing style. The action of enveloping your opponent's blade with fourth – counter-fourth without intending to parry has only one objective: to offer the sixth side (upper, outer quadrant) as a tempting target, while making other possibilities less attractive. And performing these movements at a short fencing distance makes it more difficult for the opponent to perform complex actions. Single disengages and single parries are accounted for and he has neither the distance nor the time to perform double feints or double parries.

The short distance makes the fencing more predictable. If my opponent does something, the chances are that it will involve my sixth side. In order to hide my intentions, the destructive parries have to be combined with movements both forwards and backwards. So I have two principal alternative reactions to any offensive action from my opponent – either a fast retreat (during which I can perform parry-ripostes or stop-thrusts) or to remain in and perform my favorite sixth – bind riposte position (a third option is to move forward in a counterattack with the same sixth – bind).

Note that I regard performing my favorite sixth – bind riposte during an offensive action from my opponent as basically the same action regardless of whether I am standing still or retreating. The point is that I only need two alternative reactions *regardless of the actions of my opponent*. This naturally helps significantly to lessen the threat from my opponent. Other observations include that I am possibly more accustomed to a very short fencing distance than my opponent and this makes a good launching pad for a relatively rare but rapid attack. Since most fencers avoided attacking me, I soon got as much as 40% of my hits from a rapid attack at a very close distance, also with a sixth bind. *It should be noted that the distance is so short that a simple advance is enough to score in this situation.*

My own favorite destructive parry is, as discussed in the previous section, a counter-fourth with the intention of performing my favorite sixth parry – bind riposte when something happens. The counter-fourth is performed over and over again in order to really force the opponent into that orbit. The main advantage is that if my riposte is properly executed, and even if my parry is avoided by his disengage (and I do not touch the blade at all!), I will always get at least a double. (As noted above, I would like to credit this move to the Hungarian Jenö Pap.)

But there are other options.

The Soviets pioneered the sixth – second move during the sixties. Their intention was to attack when they found the blade, with a sixth parry – bind riposte similar to mine, or a very strong beat second – disengage attack. These attacks would end in the high line. Alternatively, they would try a second – bind attack ending in the low line.

A third option was counter-second with the intention of forcing the opponent into the high line (this is not always the case with counter-fourth). Again the intention was to perform a sixth parry – bind riposte.

A fourth option was counter-sixth with the intention of making a second parry – bind riposte when something happened.

The Soviets always performed their actions in two motions: First they controlled the opponent's blade and then they scored. During this procedure, they made an advance-lunge or a fleche. Because they always needed two actions with the arm and legs, they could not initiate their movements from a short distance. The weak points (HP's) of their game were therefore twofold:

they needed the opponent's blade and they needed normal fencing distance. These weaknesses were ruthlessly exploited to beat them.

The way I did it was to fence with

1. Short fencing distance (preventing their compound actions)
2. No-blade strategy (preventing their binds)
3. Repeated steering with repeated seconds (excluding low attacks from them and steering all of their actions into the high line, my AoE.

The following principles are common to all destructive parries:

They limit the choices of your opponent and force him into your own AoE. They are performed over and over again to really force him into a predefined "orbit".

The reaction when something happens is predefined.

All are normally performed at short distance to further restrict your opponent's choices to a minimum. (As described elsewhere, the use of destructive parries, especially in combination with a short fencing distance, assumes that the fencer has a rapid weapon arm extension speed.)

6.2 Confusing Parries

A variety of parries designed to upset your opponent can be called "confusing parries." These parries have only one objective: to confuse your opponent. Eric and I developed them for a specific target: Philippe Riboud of France. Philippe is probably the most talented fencer ever from a classical point of view. At his peak, he could at disengage out of any two (and sometimes three) successive parries. In order to parry him you had to take at least three smart parries – and even then you were not safe. He moved like a cat and he was left-handed. He was also taller than I. He mostly fenced with a French grip that he could hold either right behind the guard or in an extended fashion. In short, he was a formidable opponent. He won 13 medals in World Championships or Olympic Games, of which four were gold.

When I returned to MIT in the fall of 1978, Eric Sollee and I started to analyze Philippe. It was totally counterproductive to try to parry him, because he disengaged out of any parrying attempt with such ease and without any hesitation, even without losing speed or precision. He was the only fencer who could freely offer the blade to his opponent in such a fashion that the opponent could easily attempt a parry. This attempt was invariably unsuccessful and actually helped Riboud.

A valid tactic against many attackers is to do nothing until very late in the action because attackers have difficulty disengaging against late parries. When the target is only a few centimeters away, most fencers have to try to hit without disengaging. Philippe was different because he never had to make that decision. He made an effortless automatic disengage even against very late parries if the need materialized. Constructive parries against Philippe were totally counterproductive.

However, there was a weak spot. In order for him to disengage, his opponent had to attempt a constructive parry, that is, with the intention of taking the blade. The aim therefore was to break the flow of his fencing.

So we designed confusing parries. When Philippe performed a feint in the high line, I would take a low parry so he had nothing to disengage out of. When Philippe performed a feint in the low line, I would take a high parry and so on.

This tactic needed very careful attention to the distance. It was essential to stay out of Philippe's considerable reach. This did, however, break up the flow of his fencing and sooner or later he would show a moment's hesitation. This provided me with the opportunity for a counterattack with a sixth bind action. (Remember that he was one of the few who even late in my career offered me the blade freely.) This was effective against Philippe and consequently I never lost to him unwillingly. Once, in a pool, when both of us had already qualified for the next round. I decided to try to beat him with constructive parries, not confusing parries. It took him about 60 seconds to destroy me.

I never used confusing parries against anybody else.

6.3 Controlling (Shortening) the Distance

A critical part of the new fencing paradigm is the concept of distance. A short distance limits the choices for both fencers. There is simply neither time nor distance to perform complex fencing phrases. Are there ways to increase the choices for one fencer, even though the fencing is performed at a very short distance? The answer is yes, under certain conditions – if a fencer combines a short fencing distance with an extremely fast retreat. The retreat then gives room for more complex fencing phrases and increases the choices for the fencer with the better retreating ability. We will, however, start with a more detailed discussion about the concept of distance.

Early on in the development of the paradigm we asked the following question: Does the fencer with the shorter fencing distance decide the distance in a bout? This is known as Sollee conjecture No. 2. This is a very reasonable assumption because, if one fencer feels that the distance is too long, he simply advances until he has achieved a suitable distance. The other fencer can naturally retreat, but he will soon come to the end of the piste. For the time being, therefore, we can conclude that the fencer with the shorter fencing distance decides the fencing distance in a bout, assuming that he can safely close the distance without getting hit. It is interesting that one of the favorite and often unchallenged pieces of advice from fencing masters down the ages has been: "Keep the distance! Don't get too close unless you are attacking." As discussed above, this is much more easily said than done. The next question is: can a fencer safely close the distance without exposing himself to too much danger?

A normal textbook advance consists of two steps. First you lift your front foot and move it forward until it touches the piste. Then you lift your back foot and move it forward until it also touches the piste to preserve the proper distance between the feet. Let us now consider a situation where your opponent launches a counterattack just as you have started to advance by lifting your front foot on your way forward. At this point you have moved all your weight on to your back foot. This means that you cannot start to retreat by lifting your back foot because all your weight is on it. You must first put down your front foot and then shift your weight on to it before you can lift your back foot to start your retreat. This means that if you are exposed to a properly executed counterattack during your advance, you will need to continue your forward movement for some time before your can start retreating. The time involved may be only a fraction of a second, but you may not be able to afford it.

The problem can be stated in other terms. When you stand in a proper en garde position, you are free to start movements either forward or backward. When you move in the classical way, your feet get intermittently disconnected, making changes of direction (from forward to backward or vice versa) more difficult. An advance is a movement from one *en garde* position to another while moving forward. From each *en garde* position you can change the direction of motion, but it is very difficult to change direction during an advance between *en garde* positions. This is the background to the difficulty of closing the distance and to the advice of fencing masters: keep the distance. This was indeed the dogma through the early 70's and was the major weakness of the thinking that we developed in 1973. Was there any solution to what we called the "change of direction" problem?

The solution was hard to find, yet actually very simple and we were very proud when we found it. First we had to overcome the strong dogma at the time that there was only one way of performing an advance (or a retreat) – the classical way. The solution was so simple that I am a bit ashamed that we did not see it right away. Since the problem was the disconnection of the feet between *en garde* positions during advances and retreats, we thought: do not disconnect the feet during these actions. Let both feet leave the piste at the same time and let them land at the same time, preserving both balance and distance between the feet.

How is this done?

Simply *bounce!*

6.3.1 Bouncing

Simply *bounce*. No need to shift the balance from one foot to the other as has to be done in classical advances and retreats. Once you land you are directly ready to launch an attack or start a retreat.

This concept of bouncing was against the fencing dogma of the time. Even after I showed its effectiveness in the spring of 1975 by getting into the top four in the World Cup competition in Heidenheim – where I got a blade through my right arm – I was nominated to neither the "A" group nor the "B" group of fencing candidates in my country *because it was felt that I needed to learn to fence without bouncing*. I qualified on points for the Swedish team for the 1976 Olympics, but was not selected. It was naturally a dreadful moment when I learned that the team took gold at the Olympics.

Let me mention another incident from my first AFLA[1] competition in 1974 in New York. Two competitors were discussing my fencing abilities and one said: "Have you ever seen a fencer who bounces?" "No," replied the other, "but then I have never seen a fencer from MIT, either."

The bouncing concept opened two new possibilities that we rapidly explored during the academic year of 1973 – 74. The first was, as discussed above, to bounce slightly forward or backward with a readiness to change the direction of motion. Another option was to bounce alternately forward *and* backward. Every bounce forward is a threat because it is so easy to launch a full-scale attack from it. It is also quite difficult for your opponent to launch a counterattack because your own natural movement following a forward bounce is a backward bounce. So we discovered that it was relatively safe to close the distance by alternate forward and backward bouncing. This was rapidly used to close the distance even further.

The second possibility was to use a bouncing start point to increase the length and speed of movement, while preserving the upper body balance of the initial classical advance or retreat. The background to this observation is the following. Classical advances and retreats are performed with little use of the toes. The

[1] The Amateur Fencers League of America. See Terminology.

speed of a standard retreat is generated by a push-off from the front heel. This severely limits the speed and length of the retreat. Imagine trying to run backward on your heels – you would not generate much speed.

Bouncing, in contrast, is essentially a movement on the toes. A push-off from the toes is naturally much more efficient than a push-off from the heels. The design of standard fencing shoes with their rather high heels also makes it a bit difficult to move on the toes. I found that volleyball shoes increased my ability to move on my toes.

In summary, a bouncing strategy allows longer and faster advances and retreats by taking off from the toes.

6.3.2 Strategic Uses of Bouncing

Used correctly, bouncing allows the fencer to delay the decision whether to advance or retreat since the feet do not have to become disconnected. In particular, a retreat can be performed from a standing-on-the-toes position, thus making it longer and faster. Bouncing makes it possible to close the distance without exposing the fencer to unnecessary risk. And, in contrast to classical fencers, bouncers have little need to shift their weight from one leg to the other.

Thus one can bounce back and forth against a classical fencer until he is forced to shift most of his weight to the back foot. At this point, the foot is what we call "fixed," that is, fastened; and he is unable to retreat. If fencing at short distance – and it is part of the new paradigm to fence at short distance whenever it is advantageous – the bouncer can easily hit the classical fencer with a straightforward action, either a short lunge or an advance with an extending arm.

I normally perform an advance when the risk is lowest for me. At least 40% of my single hits were scored in this way during the latter part of my career, when my style was known and opponents were understandably hesitant to commit to attacks.

The beauty of this approach is that my advance is performed from a jump forward. My intentions are hidden until the very end because, it should be remembered, my main strategy is to steer my opponent's attack into my AoE. Most of the time, I jump back after jumping forward, so my advance following a forward jump comes as a surprise. Another advantage is that an opponent with a fixed back foot is forced to extend his arm towards my upper body because he has neither the time nor the distance to do anything else. And this action is an extension into my AoE, allowing me to perform my favorite sixth parry – bind riposte. So this strategy is just another way of forcing my opponent into my AoE.

Further strategic uses of bouncing and short distance fencing include the blocking of attacks from fencers with superior technique. These fencers often like to attack from normal fencing distance so that they pick up speed before their opponent has a chance to cope with the attack. The attack is often compound, with two tempos or more.

One example of such an attack is the Soviet AoE, the sixth – second game, in which the fencer attempts to bind the blade in sixth during an advance, his opponent disengages, and the Soviet fencer beats the blade into second and fleches. Because it is a compound attack, the Soviet fencer not only needs to find the blade, but to have time and space enough to fully execute the moves.[1] In addition, the Soviet fencer needs the element of surprise, in order to make his opponent try to retreat and disengage. In this case, OP is in trouble.

The HP's for the Soviet fencer to execute this attack are the following:

1) Normal fencing distance, so as to have room to make a compound attack,
2) OP stands still (fixed back foot) or starts to move backwards,
3) OP holds the blade in a position that offers the possibility of a bind attempt,
4) OP attempts to disengage.

---

[1] The Soviets could also do the reverse against a fencer with a low line guard, initially taking the blade in second and then, if the opponent disengages, executing a sixth bind attack in the high line.

So let us take away all the hidden prerequisites. Let us fence with a short distance, take away the blade and make a direct counterattack when the attack comes. Believe me, it works beautifully. The lesson learned is that a short fencing distance makes compound attacks unattractive. Naturally, by bouncing you can delay the start of your retreat, and with the increased speed you can retreat out of reach at will.

6.4 Compulsive Push-backers and the Fixed Back Foot

I would like at this point to make a short digression from the new paradigm proper and consider the concept of the fixed back foot from the point of view of general fencing knowledge. Let me begin with a simple observation.

Many fencers respond to a surprise bind attempt by pushing back at the binding blade, resisting the pressure. For example, if you try to bind in sixth and you manage to surprise the opponent, he might instinctively resist by pushing back in sixth. If you try to surprise him by binding him in fourth, he might resist instinctively by pushing back in fourth. If he resists in this way every time that he is surprised with a bind, we may call him a compulsive push-backer. I believe that some 80% of all fencers can be made into compulsive push-backers if they are properly surprised. This means that they can be maneuvered into becoming more predictable.

So far, this is nothing out of the ordinary, and the way to handle this common situation has been studied in standard fencing books. What is interesting from my point of view is this: *Compulsive push-backers have a strong tendency to fix their back foot while they are compulsively pushing back.* This is of tremendous interest, since this is one of the few properties of an unknown fencer that can be safely and easily evaluated during the bout. You just push on the blade to feel the opponent out. If he pushes back most times, chances are that he might be a compulsive push-backer. Then you have another means of fixing the opponents back foot. I try very hard to train my students not to be compulsive push-backers, but this seems to be very difficult, for the compulsive resisting profile appears to be created early in the fencers' careers and is thus difficult for the coach to alter.

6.5 Scoring Considerations

6.5.1 The Weapon Arm

We have previously discussed the care needed to avoid giving the blade to your opponent unnecessarily.

The attentive reader might at this point ask, *how can I score a hit without risking giving away my blade?*

The answer is that *you cannot, and your attempt to score provides the moment when you are vulnerable.*

Consider the possibilities:

1) As long as the weapon arm is in the process of extending, the risks are not insurmountable, assuming that the distance is correct. Once the weapon arm is fully extended, the risk is highest that your opponent may parry or bind your blade and subsequently score.

2) However, scoring attempts with an arm that is not fully extended also involve risks: if your opponent has a fully extended arm, while yours is bent, he may score with a stop thrust.

3) Therefore, *the least risky way to score is to hit precisely at the moment when the weapon arm has become fully extended.* (I think that this should be obvious to most fencers.)

The conclusion: in order to maximize scoring opportunities, at least in epee, *a fencer should have an explosive extending motion of the weapon arm.* This is even more important if you follow the ideas in this book and take advantage of close distance fencing.

I have been amazed that, throughout my fencing career, I have never seen anybody training specifically to develop this explosiveness of the weapon arm. Top fencers train to develop technique, footwork, leg explosiveness, general strength and endurance, but rarely weapon arm extension speed. (I have special exercises for my own students to increase weapon arm explosiveness, which I discuss later.)

There are two different approaches to risk avoidance during the scoring process in epee. The basic approach is, as previously discussed, to perform scoring attempts at the exact moment when your weapon arm has become fully extended and, you hope, your opponent's has not. When fencing at close distance, this is most often achieved by a rapid retreat when your opponent makes an offensive action, or by making an offensive action yourself.

The second approach focuses on your opponent with the primary objective of making sure that his weapon arm is not extended. This is normally done through a counterattack into his offensive action, when he expects some sort of defensive action and/or retreat. This tactic is particularly suitable against an opponent with superior technique because it denies him the time and distance to use it. It goes without saying that an explosive extension of the weapon arm is advantageous for this second scoring approach.

I liked to use both approaches, my counterattack being especially deadly. I also had the speed, even from a short distance, to retreat quickly away from my opponent.

In short, this gave me three possibilities at close distance:

a)   Retreat in a balanced way with the aim of scoring at the moment my weapon arm became fully extended,

b)   Counterattack with the aim of scoring at the moment when my opponent's weapon arm was bent,

c)   The coward's way – retreat away from all scoring possibilities, both for my opponent and me.

6.5.2 Point Hit Speed and the "Critical Gap"

Let us observe the way a point approaches the opponent and scores. Assume, for the time being, that the opponent is standing still and that we aim to hit him in the chest. It is seldom difficult to get to within 10 – 15 centimeters (4 – 6 inches) or so of the target. (This is partly because most experienced fencers avoid making parries too early, since early reactions are easy to overcome.)

So far, so good. But there is considerable difficulty in moving your point across that last 10 –15 centimeters. This distance is what we can call the "critical gap," since crossing it is critical for scoring your hit and nearly everything of importance for the scoring process happens during this period.

The crossing of this gap can be executed in two ways. You can cross the gap as fast as possible, calculating that your speed may do the trick and you might score. Alternatively, you can cross more slowly, letting your opponent react, and then react to his reaction. For example, you might let him take a parry so that you can disengage, you might feint scoring towards one part of your opponent (say the high line) and then score somewhere else (for example, the foot).

Let us now observe how classical fencers are instructed to score on the offensive. The weapon arm extends during the advance in order to be fully extended when the lunge begins. Consequently, a fast advance often results in a fast weapon arm extension and a slow advance in a slow weapon arm extension; in other words, the arm and feet are connected. The primary objective is that the weapon arm should be fully extended when the advance is finished. This connection of arm and feet naturally makes the fencing more predictable.

But now let us observe the speed of the point during this theoretical exercise. First it moves with the speed of the feet (foot speed). Added to this, it moves with the speed of the weapon arm extension (arm speed). The absolute speed of the point relative to the floor or an unmoving opponent is thus the sum of the foot speed and the arm speed. Now, most of the time, the arm can move faster than the foot, making the point speed more dependent on the arm speed than the foot speed. It is also clear that the point speed will be very fast during the extend – advance.

But what happens when you cannot extend any more (when the arm is fully extended)? Then the point speed naturally drops to the foot speed. With a little bit of luck, you have managed to get your point to the beginning of the critical gap. But now you have to *slow down your point speed* just when you need it most! You are forced to try to score through the critical gap with a point speed no faster than your foot; in short, with a low absolute point hit speed. It is also clear that your extend – advance with a high point speed may cause your opponent to respond with a retreat, making your already slow point hit speed even slower with respect to the target that is now moving away from you. The relative point hit speed is thus related to the movement of the target (your opponent). This reduces your already low absolute point hit speed as you cross the critical gap to a relative point hit speed that is even slower and might approach zero. You are in trouble.

The alternative to this dilemma is to try to hit with high relative point hit speed. This means in reality that you have to wait to extend your arm fully until you can score. You must then score at the moment when your weapon has been fully extended. With a high relative point hit speed you cross the critical gap in the shortest possible time, giving your opponent little time to react.

As seen elsewhere in this book, I always tried to score with the highest possible relative point hit speed. And I did this by getting my opponent to move forward or at least have a fixed back foot when I tried to hit him, and trying to hit him during the extension of my weapon arm or right after it was fully extended. In training I did a lot of footwork and specific arm extension exercises (armwork).

Finally, scoring with a high relative point hit speed requires the arm extension to be independent of any foot movements. Arm and foot movements need to be disconnected. This was naturally part of my everyday exercises. One example is that I never practiced footwork while holding a weapon because I didn't want to risk moving my weapon in coordination with my feet, thus connecting foot and arm. (It is difficult to disconnect arm and feet and even more difficult to score with a high relative point hit speed, but difficulties are there to be overcome!)

In summary, classical fencers often score touches with a low relative point hit speed, sometimes approaching zero, while the new paradigm attempts to score with a high point hit speed.

This is probably the most difficult feature of the new paradigm. Don't try it unless you are an advanced fencer!

If you don't perform them correctly – the arm independent of the legs, the attack begun with a bent arm – these movements will cause you to run into your opponent's point with your arm still bent. This is why classical training emphasizes the full extension of the arm before the start of the final lunge and discourages bent-arm attacks.

Still, even if you do not completely agree with the rest of this book, a faster weapon arm extension and a higher point hit speed can be helpful in many situations.

6.5.3 The Scoring Process Described Mathematically

When I have presented these concepts to an audience, some of the listeners have found the scoring process difficult to understand. Some of them have benefited from modeling the concept in mathematical terms. The following description is an attempt to explain chapter 6.5.2 in mathematical terms and should be read together with that chapter. The non-mathematical reader can also benefit from some of the concepts advanced here!

Relative point speed:

$$v_p = v_a + v_f + v_{fo} \qquad (1)$$

where

v_p = Relative point velocity (relative point speed): the velocity of your point relative to your opponent's target.

v_a = Arm velocity: the speed contribution of your arm extension to the point speed

v_f = Foot velocity: the speed contribution of your footwork to the point speed

v_{fo} = Opponent's *forward* velocity: speed of your opponent, primarily foot speed, toward you.

Positive v_p, v_a, v_f indicate forward motion, while negative v_p, v_a, v_f indicate backward motion. Positive v_{fo} indicates that the opponent *is coming towards* you, thus shortening the distance. Negative v_{fo} indicates a retreat of your opponent.

Setting $v_{fo} = 0$ transforms equation (1) to the equation for absolute point speed.

If we apply equation (1) to the critical gap for scoring, then the equation describes the *relative point hit speed*.

It is generally true that a fast arm extension is faster than the fastest footwork, thus

$$v_a > v_f \qquad (2)$$

and few scoring attempt are preformed with a bending (retracting) arm so

$$v_a \geq 0 \qquad (3)$$

Using equation (1), the relative point hit speed can be characterized as follows:

Super high relative point hit speed: v_a, v_f and v_{fo} are all positive. The point moves through the critical gap very quickly. Happens rarely. When it happens, none of the fencers has a chance of reacting.

High relative point hit speed: v_a and v_f are positive while v_{fo} is zero (fixed back foot). Alternatively, v_a and v_{fo} are positive and $v_f = 0$. Parrying or disengaging are rarely possible due to lack of time.

Moderate relative point hit speed: v_a and v_{fo} are positive and v_f is negative. You are retreating during your extension. Parrying or disengaging could be possible. Alternatively, v_a and v_f are positive while v_{fo} is negative (opponent is retreating). For this alternative to be possible, you have to wait with your extension until you try to score. Most fencers extend the arm too early so that the *relative point hit speed* does not benefit from the arm extension. Parrying or disengaging could be possible when you try to score with moderate *relative point hit speed*.

Low relative point hit speed: v_f is positive while v_a and v_{fo} are zero. This is the classical fencing attack where the arm is fully extended well before any scoring attempt. In this case, the opponent has a fastened back foot. Here the opponent has time for a parry and you probably need to disengage.

Alternatively, v_{fo} is positive while v_a and v_f are zero. The classical stop thrust. The opponent runs into your point. Your arm is extended before the point reaches the critical gap.

Super low relative point hit speed: v_f is positive while $v_a = 0$ and v_{fo} is negative. The opponent has started to retreat, thus transforming a high or medium *relative point hit* speed scoring attempt into a super low. v_f is negative while $v_a = 0$ and v_{fo} are positive. The opponent has started to retreat on your attack which gives him the possibility of parrying and scoring with a higher *relative point hit speed*.

The discussion can also be summarized in Table 1, below, or in graph form, as in Figure 3 on the following page.

It would be interesting to learn by scientific measurement exactly how fast an elite fencer's arm can extend and how fast his feet can carry him. To my knowledge, there has not been any complete study attempting to assess these interesting parameters. We can, however, get some idea from the small study by Williams and Walmsley. (See the bibliography in the Appendix.). They showed in three New Zealand foil fencers that the mean arm extension speed was 6 m/sec (13.16 mph) over 60 centimeters, or just under two feet in one tenth of a second. (The maxi-

Table 1
Relative point hit speed crossing the critical gap

Relative point hit speed (v_p)	v_a	v_f	v_{fo}	Sum
Super High	++	+	+	4 plus
High	++	0	+	3 plus
High	++	+	0	3 plus
Medium	++	-	+	2 plus
Medium	0	+	+	2 plus
Low	0	+	0	1 plus
Low	0	0	+	1 plus
Super Low	0	+	-	0-1 plus

Notes: No foot movement from either fencer means no chance of scoring, an isolated arm extension without any forward motion probably will not hit unless OP is not retreating, and attacking with a retracting arm will probably not succeed. These theoretical possibilities are therefore not included in the table. The relationships of Table 1 can also be expressed as the graph on the following page.

mal arm extension speed that would correspond to the point hit speed in resting conditions would naturally be higher.)

Williams and Walmsley did not measure mean foot speed directly, but it is possible from other data they presented to indirectly assess the mean foot speed over a 40-centimeter distance to be around 2 m/sec. (This result requires certain assumptions, the most important being that the arm extension speed is independent of the food speed, which has not been shown.)

The mean arm extension speed appears to be approximately *3 times* the mean foot speed. Even if the difference in ratio between the maximal arm extension speed and the maximal foot speed is

Figure 3
Graph: Relative point speed of fencer and OP

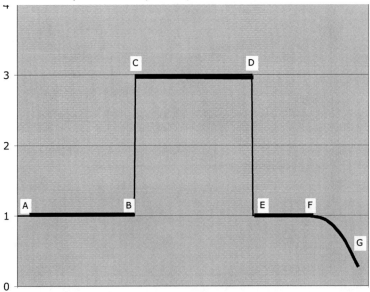

Time

In this example, the fencer is continuously advancing towards OP. Initially, OP is not moving. The point speed is equal to the foot speed between point A and B. Between point C and D the fencer is extending the arm as well as advancing. At point D the arm is fully extended. Point D is therefore the optimal point to score with a high relative hit speed. After point D the point speed drops back to the foot speed between point E and F. At point F the opponent starts retreating and the relative point speed drops even further.

less than that, our assumption, in the tables presented earlier in this chapter, that the arm extension speed is approximately twice that of the foot speed appears to be reasonably conservative.

From Figure 3 the following advantages may be anticipated from a fast retreat. First, we would get more time to react. More importantly, OP's relative point hit speed should go down dramatically, since he will have completed his extension without scoring, and we are already moving backwards.

(Please note that this might not happen with all opponents: for example, I would expect Pavel Kolobkov to go after you with a bent arm, delaying his extension until a time when he has a possibility of scoring.)

6.6 The Ideal Opponent

It is worth spending some time looking at the overall prerequisites of an opponent. Is it possible that the detailed and actually rather simple advice given in this section only works against a few selected opponents? Another way of addressing this question is to describe the overall hidden prerequisites that I need from an opponent.

The principal HP (the minimum) is that my opponent takes, or can be provoked to take the classical en garde position with his blade pointing toward me.

There are two additional *facilitating* HP's that are not critical but would be helpful. These are

1) OP can be provoked to extend his weapon arm in the *en garde* position at least half-way, and

2) OP does not bounce or, if he does, at least bounces up and down rather than back and forth. (When he moves, he moves with normal classical advances and retreats.)

Our principal HP (blade pointed at me) will enable us to initiate blade-to-blade contact at our own choosing, assuming that we elect to use the no-blade strategy as discussed previously. Many fencers who do not have a classical en garde can be provoked into adopting one if we just seem threatening enough. This means that we have the opportunity to seek blade contact at will, while our opponent cannot. He will only be able to get blade contact when we let him. This is very frustrating for him and might provoke him into doing something adventurous that we can use to our advantage.

If we can get the first facilitating HP (half-extended arm) in addition, the room to maneuver increases tremendously. The first facilitating HP allows us to take sixth parry – bind at will with the advantages previously described.

The second facilitating HP (no bouncing) is a bit less obvious. Our advantage comes because OP has trouble changing his direction of motion (from forwards to backwards or vice versa). When moving forward, OP must begin by shifting his weight to the back foot, thereby "fixing" it (fastening it to the floor) as discussed earlier. Thus the second facilitating hidden prerequisite means that we may fasten the opponent's back foot whenever we want. And if we use bouncing tactics at a short distance, we can elect to counterattack at will. When our opponent advances, then, we have these options:

1) Retreat without any action,
2) Retreat with stop thrust, parry-riposte, or parry – bind,
3) Counterattack with a parry – bind.

Thus, if we can get both facilitating hidden prerequisites, OP will be very easy to beat.

I introduced the new paradigm in its fully developed form on the world-class fencing stage during the 1976 – 77 season. At this point, most opponents gave me, by default, both the principal and the two facilitating HP's. The classical weapon arm position was half-extended, and bouncing was unheard-of.

This was a fun time in my fencing career. I, an unknown Swedish fencer without any success during my junior years, suddenly beat everybody in the world. I have described these years from a personal angle in an earlier chapter.

Unfortunately, since those days, most top fencers have adopted most of the strategies discussed in this book. The result is that many bouts turn into a game of "chicken," with both fencers using similar strategies and only waiting for mistakes by their opponent. You will see very few fencing phrases in these bouts.

This is another reason for the lack of classical epee fencing at the world-class level.

6.7 The Difficult Opponent

Difficult opponents are the converse of ideal opponents: they are the fencers who do not give any of the hidden prerequisites as described earlier. These fall into two categories:

1) Those who adopt the strategies described in this book,
2) Those who fence with a French handle and hold the weapon by the pommel. (We can call these fencers French handlers or pommelers.)

It is difficult to fence against somebody with a similar strategy because they can anticipate all your tactical maneuvers. Either you can decide to be the person in this chicken game who adheres most strictly to the new fencing paradigm – which will result in fencing at very close distance – or you take a chance with an independent attack from close range. Since I was the first one to introduce the new paradigm and it took three years for my opponents to copy my strategy, I mainly adhered to it. In 1980 a few fencers began to copy my strategy (mainly the Poles) and it was in that year, after winning the Olympics, that I elected to stop fencing on the world-class stage.

The French-handlers are a different story, since they constituted a major problem for me throughout my career. Successful French-handlers never give the blade and thus withhold from me the principal hidden prerequisite (classical *en garde*) and one of the two facilitating hidden prerequisites (half-extended weapon arm). In addition, they have a much longer reach when they extend, since they are holding the weapon by the pommel. Their strategy is to do very little; but once something begins to happen, they like to maneuver in such a way that the fight develops into a "Who has the longest arm?" competition. Remember that I was (and still am) only 1.79 m (5' 10") tall. This situation meant that only one of the two scoring options remained open for me (see section 6.5, "Scoring considerations"). I needed to concentrate on scoring when my opponent's arm was not fully extended. To concentrate on scoring at the moment when my own arm was fully extended would mean entering a "Who has the longest arm?" competition, which I would never win.

Many strong classical fencers do not have a problem with French handlers. They simply try to bind the blade to provoke a reaction. This forces the French-handlers to do something – to counterattack direct, by disengage, or by a series of disengages. The advanced classical fencer can then make one or more parries and then riposte. The threat of this classical parry-riposte forces the French handler into inactivity and opens him to a straight attack from the classical fencer. If the French handler extends his arm, he is immediately parried.

I did not have the talent for this classical strategy in its traditional form, with successive parries during a compound attack, so French-handlers remained a tremendous challenge. My solution was to explore the remaining facilitating hidden prerequisite still open to me: the lack of bouncing from my opponent. So my strategic and tactical considerations included the following:

1) Very short distance
2) Vigorous work with the weapon arm to force my opponent into my own AoE. Since most French-handlers want to hit low, you take vigorous low destructive parries to force him high into your own AoE and away from his. (If a French handler prefers to hit high, you might consider forcing him low or blocking him high with your guard as you attempt to hit him.)
3) Vigorous bouncing back and forth to get my opponent moving with classical retreats and advances and thus open themselves to a counterattack.

These tactics were not easy, and in fact I lost most of these bouts – with the exception of the very important bouts in championships when all the hits could be categorized as Olympic touches. In those situations, the actions become more predictable and favored the fencer with the clearer strategy.

This chapter would not be complete without mentioning that Alexander (Alex) Pusch and Philippe Riboud were also very difficult fencers for different reasons. I never lost a crucial bout to either of them, but they both forced me to perform at my very best. To beat Philippe, I even had to develop new tactics (see 6.2, "Confusing Parries.")). Alex is discussed elsewhere. Alex and Philippe won at least 26 Olympic and World Championship medals.

I must also mention my teammate Rolf Edling (World Champion in 1973 and 1974 and runner-up in 1977) as a difficult opponent, since his style was difficult for me to handle and he beat me in some competitions, especially early in my career. As I have already mentioned, I was able to defeat him only when it was supremely important to me, notably in the World Championship and Olympic finals.

7.

Björne Väggö on the New Paradigm

In this chapter I will give my personal thoughts, based on my own experience of the new paradigm.

To start with, some background. Johan and I belong to that generation of Swedish fencers who came after the great names of the 70's. Men like Edling, von Essen, Jacobson, Flodström and Högström were well respected and well known in the international fencing community. This meant that we younger fencers had an excellent training environment, being part of the Swedish "B" squad at the time. Both Johan and I trained in clubs other than those attended by the "permanent members" of the national team mentioned above. Johan was born in 1954 and I in 1955, in Stockholm and Göteborg (Gothenburg) respectively. The training camps we attended with the national team included fencing bouts, footwork, lessons and all kinds of physical training. So we enjoyed the privilege of training with some of the top fencers in the world.

But there were no organized discussions about fencing strategy. Although we were in the best physical and technical training environment, our results would not have been as successful as they were had we not worked, learned and reflected over epee fencing strategy and tactics. The new paradigm made all the difference, enabling us to reach the top with limited technique.

Johan and I met for the first time as teenagers when competing at a national level as juniors in Sweden. We got to know each other better during our military service in 1974 – 75, when we both participated in a special sports program for talented athletes. We fenced approximately twice a week Monday through Friday (plus regular practice or competitions during the weekends), the remaining time being spent on regular military service tasks, such as carrying backpacks, cleaning rifles and sleeping in tents. Thus began a period when we spent many days together in training camps and competitions around the world. Like Johan, I started to think about strategies and tactics, but it was only after the 1980 Olympics that we combined our experiences in a deeper way. Because he had retired, it was probably easier for Johan to put his thoughts into words. I had four more years to train and develop my fencing skills for the 1984 Olympics in Los Angeles. Undoubtedly my career really kicked off after I got a better understanding of the strategic and tactical dimension of fencing. Johan has been a great inspiration in this respect. I had some good results before 1980, like becoming the NCAA champion for the University of Notre Dame in 1978 and a member of the Swedish national team in 1979 (I did not, however, qualify for the Moscow Olympics), but it was really after 1980 that I reached a deeper understanding of the new paradigm and my results became competitive on a world-class level. I became Swedish champion and World University champion in 1981 and won a silver medal at the 1984 Olympics.

I will try to describe my thoughts about strategy and tactics and how they developed over time using the terminology presented in this book.

7.1 Bouncing

Like Johan, I adopted the bouncing technique early on. Since then, bouncing has always been fundamental to my strategy and tactics. It made it possible to close or open up the distance to my opponent. It is easy to attack from a forward bounce and at the same time, not that easy for the opponent to launch a counter-attack, because a backward bounce is a natural movement following a forward bounce. I used this foot mechanism for all my actions. This naturally required excellent physical fitness, speed and strength in the legs, feet and toes. I ended all training sessions with footwork exercises and spent many hours on them, although in a more classic way than Johan. In addition, on Friday evenings, when my club had no regular practice sessions, I dedicated Friday evening practice just to footwork.

In this way, I developed two complementary world-class footwork movements that were the basis for my AoE: I was able to retreat very quickly or could execute a fleche attack at any given moment. My strategy was to put pressure on my opponent by bouncing forward. This bouncing was purposely somewhat irregular with the objective of pressurizing my opponent into attacking me. I usually then retreated, or else I counterattacked at the same moment that my opponent attacked me. I chose whether to retreat or counterattack depending on my previous experience with my opponent and the match situation (Olympic or non-Olympic touches). I even sometimes just relied on my inner senses without thinking which option to take.

7.2 Area of Excellence

My experience in the field of AoE is quite different from Johan's, although the fundamental thinking was and is very similar. The term AoE did not exist for me early in my career. But I used the concept actively, employing two different perspectives, my own and my opponent's. I started to document my thinking in the late 70's in a little black booklet. I wrote about the tactical and technical strengths of each fencer on the World Cup circuit, as well as describing each key hit. I added data as I met individual fencers in different tournaments over a period of 10 years from 1974 to 1984. There were two headings for each fencer in my black book:

- The strengths of my opponent
- The tactics I should use

Looking back and using this book's terminology, I now realize that I systematically tracked my opponent's AoE. This is in line with one of Johan's main points as a basis for fencing strategy.

My own AoE was made up of very simple movements. Bouncing was the basis for all my actions. Johan's AoE was the sixth parry-riposte as a counterattack movement. My technical strength did not rely on parries, even though I used them quite effectively. My AoE was simply to disengage out of an attack, preferably compound, from my opponent.

I combined this with a stop hit while retreating. Often I scored by hitting my opponent's hand or arm. I developed a stop hit technique allied to an ability to angulate my blade and guard in such a way that it became difficult or impossible for my opponent to score. We normally call this move "opposition."

I also employed blocking. The word describes defensive arm actions besides traditional blade-to-blade parrying. These actions include (but are not limited to) actions such as deflecting the incoming point or blade with the guard alone or locking the opponent's guard or the weapon arm with the guard. For example, if an opponent attacked me in the high line, where I might normally consider taking a sixth parry, I would begin to extend my arm into his attack and at the moment when he was about to hit, my arm would be fully extended, and my guard would deflect his blade just enough for his point to miss its target. This was not a parry; I just blocked the opponent's point and blade with my guard

I also developed considerable skill against attacks in all lines, especially in the high lines and from opponents attempting to engage in fourth or sixth. Often I scored single hits with this world-class move, which was my preferred approach in Olympic touch situations. Needless to say, the extension of my weapon arm was very rapid.

As a junior, I executed this hit primarily as a defensive movement, but it was not effective when my opponent took an early lead and decided to wait for me to attack. In my late junior years I began training to execute this movement as an attack in countertime.

I worked enormously hard to develop my fleche technique to complement the defensive side of my AoE. This both broadened my repertoire of moves and made it easier for me to alter my tactics. By putting pressure on my opponent through a well-developed bouncing technique and close fencing distance, I could either quickly retreat or counterattack. The fleche attack was executed in the same way with one or two simple disengages or just a straight attack in countertime. The disengages could go in any direction: from high to high, i.e. sixth − fourth, or from high to low, i.e. sixth – eighth. In this way I wanted to be unpredictable to my opponents. I used the bouncing technique to move my opponent into my AoE and, in parallel with Johan's experience, I found that defensive and offensive movements were very much alike.

7.3 Non-Olympic Touches

Even though most of my hits were based on a simple stop hit, a disengage with opposition, and a fleche attack with disengage, I decided to develop some other scoring moves if my tactics did not work. This was especially necessary against fencers with an extended arm, whom I tended to engage in the low line by a seventh or eighth bind parry-riposte, or in countertime. But I never used these moves in Olympic touch situations, when I relied solely on my AoE.

7.4 Hidden Prerequisites

The concept of hidden prerequisites was an eye-opener for me that really kick-started my fencing career. Once again, this term did not exist at the time, but with the help of Johan I understood the concept and was able to practice it with a lot of success. It really all happened while preparing for the World University Games in Bucharest, Romania, in 1981. Both Johan and I were there to fence in individual and team events. We trained in the gymnasium a week before the individual competition.

The Soviet top fencer Ticho was also there and he invited me to fence a couple of bouts. Ticho was very athletic and at the same time technical, like most Soviets at national team level. I lost the training bouts by wide margins.

Johan immediately came up to me when the session was over and said: "Try to close the distance. And take away your blade: lower it to the floor."

My first thought was that it would be "strange and scary" to move close in on a very athletic world-class fencer, especially with my blade not pointing at my opponent. It did not sound logical, but I was eager to try. I found that it was a totally different game.

The bout became very even. I simply made a direct counterattack with or without a disengage at the same moment he started his attack. Ticho's prerequisite was to engage my blade and this was not possible if it was pointing at the floor. Remember Johan's analysis throughout Chapter 6 of the tactics to use against Soviet fencers, which we can summarize as follows: "Let us take away all their hidden prerequisites. Let us fence at short distance, remove the blade and make a direct counterattack when their attack comes." I had taken away Ticho's hidden prerequisite. Now I understand that I had started to practice and learn a new way of thinking and acting on the piste. This was the moment I started to use the new paradigm in a broader sense.

7.5 The World University Games, 1981

The World University Games were a true success story for me. In my first direct elimination bout, I had to fence Olivier Carrard from Switzerland, a former European champion and a very competitive fencer. Tactically, I used a mixture of my preferred AoE counterattacks and stop hits. My tactics and timing worked very well and I won. Then I had to meet three Soviet fencers, Dunaiev, Kondogo and Mojaev, in succession to reach the final. Mojaev had won the silver medal at the World Championships two weeks earlier, and all of them were members of their national team. This was the first time that I fully applied the new paradigm in competition. The tactical choice was the same in all three bouts. I lowered my blade so that my opponents could not engage it, I shortened the fencing distance, and I steered the fencing into my AoE so that I could use my counterattacks into their preparations. It was a wonderful feeling to change from having a really hard time to winning bouts against Soviet fencers and feeling in control of the game. My self-confidence naturally increased match by match.

In addition, I found that it was a big advantage to have superior skills in close combat situations, as Johan has already pointed out. After hundreds of bouts with Johan where he always shortened the distance to overcome my stop hit advantage, my close combat skills had considerably improved. This helped me on the road to victory in this championship.

I fenced Olivier Lenglet of France in the final. He was a very good attacker and could move extremely fast from almost standing still to a full-speed fleche attack. True to the Olympic touch situation, we both fenced within our AoE in the final, but when he fleched at me, he was inside my AoE. Despite his speed, my footwork was good enough for me to retreat and use my number one AoE, the simple stop hit.

This victory was valuable preparation for the Olympics three years later.

7.6 The Los Angeles Olympics, 1984

My learning experience during the World University Games had been profound. The concept of hidden prerequisites had raised me to the podium and to a totally new level of strategic awareness. I continued to work hard on my footwork and my AoE of stop hit and fleche counterattack with a simple disengage in all lines. My national team trainer, Orwar Jönsson, did a wonderful job of refining the technical execution and timing of these very basic movements. He worked very much in line with the new paradigm. We focused on my AoE and ignored the traditional approach of developing long complex and combined series of movements. Orwar even acted as my main opponent when giving lessons. This sharpened my skills against specific opponents during the Olympics.

It is worth noting that the Swedish national team at these Olympics was very much in harmony and we had a good team spirit among fencers as well as leaders. Our problem was that we had a reputation to live up to. Remember that from 1973 to 1980 Swedish fencers had won five World Championship or Olympic team medals, four of them gold, and six individual medals: four gold, one silver and one bronze – unbelievable results for a country whose population was then barely over 8,000,000. These results created high expectations and generated quite a lot of pressure from the media.

I mentioned earlier about fencing the Soviets at very short distance. During the Olympics, I did the opposite in one situation. I had to fence Lenglet in my first direct elimination fight. He had developed a lot since 1981 and, after an excellent season, was already the World Cup winner for 1984. He took an early lead using his favorite fleche attack, the fastest in the world. I had to change something as I was losing, so I decided to increase the fencing distance by about a foot. Olivier continued with his previously successful fleche attacks, but now from too long a distance. This gave me more time to see the attacks coming and to react with my stop hit. I had moved him into my AoE. I think I made six straight hits on his arm in the second half of the bout! He probably remembered the World University Games and maybe became nervous, particularly as he had a lot of pressure on him from the French federation.

I was lucky that he obviously had not heard about the second Sollee conjecture: the fencer with the shorter fencing distance decides the distance in the bout. He could easily have shortened the distance before committing to an attack, but he did not notice that I had increased the fencing distance, most likely due to nervousness.

In my second DE bout, I met Angelo Mazzoni from Italy, who had beaten me 5 – 0 in the pool the previous day and had collected another three 5 – 0 victories. He used a French handle and was an extremely talented fencer. I think it was quite an advantage for me to have lost the day before, as it made him overconfident, while I had nothing to lose. In addition, the direct elimination was definitely an Olympic touch situation. I fenced very much according to the new paradigm. I had to move extremely close to reduce Mazzoni's advantage in length, and I had to forget the classic guard position, since he was very accurate to the hand. It was a quick bout. I took an early lead, so Mazzoni had to attack me, which he did over and over again, thereby fencing within my AoE. I could counterattack or make double hits on his attacks. I do not remember every hit, but he equalized at the very end and we came to a 9– all situation. Then he tried a coupé attack to my arm, but I relied on my preferred move in Olympic touch situations – that simple stop hit – which was working extremely well that day. I hit him on the hand.

In the quarter-final I had to fence Elmar Bormann, the reigning World Champion. My trainer had imitated him during lessons. Elmar had a very special and unique fencing style, seeking the blade from a series of extremely quick hand and arm movements, normally using sixth and second engagements in what some called a frantic windshield-wiper action. He ended up engaging the blade high or low and making a quick fleche attack. His first two or three movements were used to get his opponent to extend the arm. My tactics were not to react at all and definitely not to extend my arm into his preparation. Instead I waited for his attack, which moved him into my AoE, before disengaging during the final part of his attack and hitting him with my world-class stop hit. It worked and I won 10 – 7.

I mentioned earlier that I logged all my main competitors' AoE and my own tactics in a little booklet. I did one more thing. I documented situations to learn from and remember. I wrote down the situation and then what to do next time it occurred. The contents of this booklet were one of the main reasons why I reached the Olympic final. One of these learning points was especially memorable.

Sweden had fenced Switzerland in a team match earlier in the 1984 season. In that match, I fenced Daniel Giger, who had been one of the top Swiss fencers for many years. In those days each team of four fenced each person in the opposing team in 5-hit bouts. Daniel and I reached 4 – all, with Switzerland needing victory more than Sweden. I had retreated to a position behind the 2-meter warning line and there were only a few seconds left. When the referee said *"Allez,"* I thought, "Let's see what happens and then decide what to do." That was why I lost the bout. Daniel, on the other hand, had decided exactly what to do: since I could not retreat, he made a fleche attack and won. I wrote in my little booklet "Never enter into a situation where there are only a few seconds left without having decided what to do."

Now, in the semifinals of the Olympics, I found myself in almost the same situation against Stefano Bellone of Italy. There were only four seconds left and I was on the 2-meter warning line leading 3 – 2. The difference this time was that I had learned from my experience of fencing Giger, and this was the decisive moment to qualify or not for the Olympic final. It was obvious that Stefano would attack, probably with a fleche. I could retreat 2 meters, but this was not a good option. There was a high probability that Stefano would overrun me, just as Daniel had done earlier in the season.

The situation became clear. I decided to meet Stefano's attack with a straight, powerful counterattack. Stefano's AoE was an attack into my fourth line. I remember how I centered my guard position almost in the middle between sixth and fourth to protect the inside of my arm from getting hit. The referee said "*Etes vous prêts? Allez!*" Stefano fleched to my fourth side and I counterattacked decisively. I counterattacked, and at the same time blocked his point and blade with my guard. I scored; Stefano missed. The score was 4 – 2 and there were only 2 seconds left, not enough time for Stefano to score twice. I was in the Olympic final!

In the final, however, I had no chance against Philippe Boisse of France. He had mastered all aspects of the game. My tactics were to rely on my preferred Olympic touch. Boisse fleched twice in the early part of the bout. My point slid along his arm but the pressure was not enough to register a hit. I was two touches behind. The fact that I was losing forced me to attack, and Philippe fenced very well tactically as time passed. In a way, you could say Philippe made me fence outside my AoE and inside his for most of the bout. The final score was 10 – 5. I was bitterly disappointed at first, but then I realized what I had done and said to myself:

"I did not lose the gold medal, I won the silver."

Above: Björne Väggö with his Olympic medal, 1984.

Below: Björne on the podium

7.7 Nervousness and Mental Training

I am a person with healthy self-esteem, but strangely, I do not have a tremendous amount of self-confidence. I have to constantly prove my capabilities to myself. My self-confidence therefore increases by winning bouts and qualifying for the next round. My level of nervousness is at its peak at the beginning of a competition and especially in the first round. I was quite aware of this and therefore mentally prepared myself to handle the first round of the Olympics over a period of 9 months prior to the Games. I practiced mental training each time I went out cross-country running. I saw myself on the piste fencing in the first pool. I pictured myself having a clear mind and basing all my movements on the tactics decided. The key for me was to create a feeling of being clear and precise in my head despite my nervousness.

I also adopted the Norwegian psychological trainer Willo Railos's way of thinking, which is: reduce negative thoughts and the fear of losing, while mobilizing positive thoughts and the will to win. I used this approach for a long time to prepare myself mentally.

There were no official world rankings at the time, but I estimate I was only around 30th in the world going into the 1984 Olympics. This meant there was no pressure from my federation or from me to bring home a medal, which of course was quite an advantage compared to Johan's situation during the 1980 Olympics. My personal goal was simply to end in the top eight.

The first day consisted of three rounds of pools, with direct elimination from 16 the following day. My feelings of nervousness decreased quite a bit after the first round of pools. From then onwards, I felt that I had nothing to lose. I felt some nervousness at the beginning of my first DE bout against Olivier Lenglet, but he was much more nervous, perhaps because of the pressure of being World Cup Champion and therefore being expected to produce. This gave me a clear advantage. My self-confidence increased with each bout that I won. Coming into the final of eight, I was calm and focused and did not feel any nervousness, as I had already performed much better than expected. I felt joy and pride, but was still hungry to win bouts. I could fence from an underdog position, with the pressure to win wholly on my opponent, and followed the mantra "There is nothing to lose and a whole lot to win."

Important for reaching my best at decisive moments were my ability to concentrate and focus when fencing, but also to relax and recover between bouts. For example, my bout with Mazzoni ended around lunchtime. The quarterfinals started at 7 o'clock in the evening. The Swedish team had rented a house in the Long Beach area and we went back for lunch. I was able to rest and sleep for about three quarters of an hour during the afternoon. These 45 minutes of sleep made me extremely alert and rested coming into my quarterfinal in the evening.

7.8 Keys for Fencing Success

The main components that enabled me to reach the Olympic final were:

- I used the bouncing technique that was my basis for all tactical considerations.
- I knew my own AoE and the AoE of my competitors.
- I could vary my fencing distance from very short to quite long.
- I documented learning experiences so that I could remember what to do when I encountered the same opponent later on in my career.
- I had the ability to switch from being totally focused in a bout situation to relaxing between bouts and rounds.

8.

Johan: My Personal Approach

Chapters 1 – 7 describe a fencing paradigm with tactics and strategy that I believe has at least some fundamental and universal applicability. The present chapter describes the way I have handled the paradigm when fencing. Geoff Pingree and Björne Väggö have discussed the paradigm from their own viewpoints in chapters 5.7 and 7. The present chapter aims to describe features that are truly personal to me and are definitely not universally applicable. They are not normally described in fencing literature and may therefore be of some general interest. I will, for example, describe how I made sure that I performed at my best when I needed to the most. *These procedures worked for me, but should not necessarily be copied.* Nevertheless, the thought process is important, and I suggest that interested fencers should ask themselves the questions I asked myself, but they should be aware that the answers could (and maybe should!) be different from mine.

8.1 To Cheat or Not to Cheat

I strongly resent cheats. Some people secretly admire those who cheat because they take risks and often get away with them. In addition, there are sometimes fuzzy borders between cheating and simply stretching the rules. Is it acceptable to cheat on the piste, if the referee does not see it?

In fencing there are a lot of fuzzy situations, like whether a hit arrives before or after the halt, or whether a fencer has one foot off the piste when he scores, and so on. If the referee wrongly awards you a hit, should you correct him?

Another question concerns actions that are against the spirit of the rules but not against how they are written. This is not a big issue for most fencers, but it caused distinct problems for me.

Because I have such a strong dislike of cheats, I did not do anything that even slightly approached the fuzzy borders. I immediately acknowledged any hits that the referee might wrongly award me. Even though I lost many hits that I might have been awarded, this was not the largest problem for me. There was another dimension: because I always tried to behave like a gentleman, I expected others to do the same. This is not the way the world works. I soon found out that not all fencers were gentlemen on the piste, especially those from the East Bloc countries. Because I got upset when others cheated and then lost my concentration, some fencers started to cheat, not to gain hits, but just to get me upset and out of balance.

It is also important to understand that fencing during the 70's was dominated by the Soviet Union and its associated satellite states. Success in sports was one of the few ways for an individual to escape the misery of his situation. Success could change the lives not only of the individual fencer, but also his whole family. East Bloc fencers were prepared to do whatever it took to win, and they had a well-prepared state supporting their efforts. (Another indication of the hard lives of Eastern bloc fencers is that they often sold their own equipment to get some hard currency to buy something that they needed to take home. I still own 50 excellent Russian blades – with points! – that I bought for $3 apiece.)

Losing bouts to get somebody out of a competition, and selling bouts, were standard procedures. A fencer with four victories in a pool of six would sell his last bout to the highest bidder, often in exchange for a bout given in return later in the competition or even at a later competition. After I became World Champion in 1977, I suddenly realized that every time I was not sure of promotion from a pool I always (and I mean always) ended up being eliminated. The direct elimination procedure from 32 fencers down to a final pool of six was introduced during the last years of the 70's, but did not stop the buying and selling of bouts in the three or four preliminary rounds. In the East, the Communist states were masters of this art; the Germans were leaders in the

West. (The present procedure of preliminary rounds where most fencers qualify and all hits count has totally eliminated this pernicious practice.)

It was always difficult to beat a Soviet fencer when the referee came from another communist country. In my last bout to get into the 1980 Olympic final I scored the last hit against a Hungarian and was very happy. The Russian referee, however, did not award the hit and gave no reason. I had to concentrate again and scored the next hit, when the same thing happened again. It was only when the referee saw that I did not intend to let my opponent get any more hits that he let me into the final.

Another standard procedure at the time was that fencers were allowed to take a 10-minute break for indisposition, such as cramp or a sore back, and 20 minutes for an injury confirmed by a doctor. As a result, many fencers who were losing took a break during the direct elimination bouts.

(I have to say that although there was a definite cheating culture in world fencing during the 1970's and 1980's, it has now largely disappeared, in part due to changes in fencing regulations, but also to the breakup of the Soviet Union and the East Bloc.)

The 1975 – 76 season was a difficult one for me, since members of my own national team would regularly give bouts to each other to keep me out. Not being selected for the Olympics despite being in the top four highlighted a number of ethical issues in my mind. In the summer of 1976, I began to face them.

What are the virtues of being ethical in an unethical world? The answer for me was a clear conscience but little fencing success.

Does it help anybody else, if I behave ethically? Maybe, if I become a role model for youngsters. However, at the time, I told myself, I was not yet a role model.

Could I ever qualify for the Swedish team, if I continued to follow my self-imposed ethical standards? The answer was definitely no.

What was my real problem – being ethical or getting upset when others were unethical? The answer was clearly the latter.

I spent that summer thinking about these issues and formulating a strategy for going forward. The first question to address was whether competitive fencing was more important than a totally clear conscience. I had to admit that fencing was very important to me, and I was not ready to stop competing just to preserve my idea of total integrity. It was also clear that it was not possible for me to qualify for the Swedish team without altering my mental attitude.

I finally settled on the following way of thinking. I had to accept that cheating was an accepted part of fencing and that opponents might take illegal substances, buy and sell bouts, and fake injuries. Referees cheated as well. The only way to preserve my balance was to recognize that the culture was as it was, but to train so hard that I beat them anyway. I would never get upset again if someone cheated. It was just part of the game. Total acceptance of the existing reality was the key.

I also had to consider my own behavior. Even if I accepted that others cheated, I did not want to cheat myself. So I reached a compromise that allowed me to be effective on the piste but still be able to look myself in the eye. I moved into the fuzzy areas between what is ethical and what is not. To buy or sell bouts was out of the question. But accepting hits that the referee wrongly awarded to me (remaining silent when my opponent complained) and even claiming indisposition when I needed a break became acceptable. I am not proud of entering these fuzzy areas with their questionable ethics, but the alternative was to stop competitive fencing altogether – and this was like letting the cheats win.

It is part of my own mental therapy that I now write these lines about when I compromised my own ethical ideals (less than others, but nevertheless to an extent).

8.2 Mental Attitude for Match Situations

The Ni To Ichi Way of strategy is recorded in the Book of the Void.

What is called the spirit of the void is where there is nothing. It is not included in a man's knowledge. Of course the void is nothingness. By knowing things that exist, you can know that which does not exist. That is the void.

....

Then you will come to think of things in a wide sense and, taking the void as the Way, you will see the Way as void.

In the void is virtue, and no evil.

—Miyamoto Musashi[1]

This is a personal section and all fencers need to find their own way to handle a match situation. What is valid for one fencer may not be valid for another. Still, my experience may be of some general interest since the reader may find it useful to ask himself (or herself) the same questions that I have, even if he finds different answers.

My situation was difficult because I became nervous in trivial situations. I have already mentioned that I could fence very well in practice until my opponent suddenly suggested that the loser of the next bout should buy the winner a beer. I always got nervous and lost!

Early in my career, I found out that I fenced better when I thought I was going to lose against better fencers but had a problem with fencers whom I should beat easily. In the latter situation, I thought that I would get an easy win. I read books about winning through visualizing victory, but unlike Björne, when I tried that I only lost.

I also found that when I thought of a sequence of actions, like "If I do A, then my opponent will do B and I will do C to score,"

---

[1] From "The Book of the Void," the fifth and final part of *The Book of the Five Rings* by Miyamoto Musashi. When I fenced at my very best, I was so focused that my mind felt like it contained "nothingness"

it did not work out at all. I fenced at my best when I did not think on an action-based level but rather on a general tactical level, such as staying out of my opponent's AoE and keeping a short distance that limited his possibilities. When actions were performed automatically, they were more effective. This means that all actions I expected to perform in a bout needed to be practiced to such an extent that they became automatic.

I developed my own strategy of mental preparation. Before a match I would repeat the following mantra over and over again to reach the right mental attitude, " My opponent is better than I am, but I will fight as hard as I can and make it as difficult as possible for him to win." This worked for me. The key was never to think the paralyzing thought that I might win, because that was close to "I should win" and "I have to win," and that thought would make me nervous. Remember that I lost my last bout in the 1980 Olympics when that thought entered my head.

Thinking my mantra was sometimes ridiculous, especially after I won the World Championship and often fenced poorer fencers. But even though it was superficially absurd, the mantra was a helpful preparation for a bout.

On one occasion, however, it guided me in the wrong direction. That was in the final of the World Championship in 1977. I was not used to the idea that I could actually reach the final and to the tremendous pressure of that environment. The use of my mantra actually caused me to be overeager, even though I was not actually nervous (I have been nervous so often that I can always identify the feeling). This overeagerness was the main reason why I lost the two first bouts. For the rest of the final I refrained from using my mantra and won the remaining six bouts.

My mantra corresponds nicely with the advice that generations of fencing masters have given their students: "Opponents come in only two types: some are good, and the rest are dangerous."

Although thinking my mantra was sufficient in most situations, thinking nothing was even better. I believe that focusing on my mantra was a bridge to help me move into the thinking–nothing state. By the end of my career (1980), I could move into the thinking–nothing state directly without the aid of my mantra. Thinking nothing, not even black, is a challenge. I meditated every day before every training session to achieve better and better mental control. I would start by thinking everyday thoughts and then move into the thinking–nothing stage, after which I let myself sleep for 30 – 60 minutes. Immediately after this procedure, I was ready to fence a very high quality training session. During numerous week-long training camps, I always shared a room with Björne Väggö. We trained three or four times a day, and we meditated and slept before nearly every training session. I think we gained a lot of mental stability from this practice.

I learned much later that other athletes use similar procedure so as not to focus on the wrong things. A Swedish tennis player who had problems winning matches, even though he played well, was advised to "think yellow" during the numerous breaks in a tennis match. It worked and he went on to become a world-class player.

Although my nervousness resulted in my being knocked out of several competitions during the preliminary rounds, if I survived it became an advantage in the latter stages. Most fencers become nervous in important situations, even if they do not admit it to themselves. My advantage in these situations was that I knew how to handle nervousness, but my opponents did not and so were more prone to make mistakes. This effect should be compared with Chapter 2's discussion of Olympic touches, where the predictability of the fencing increases.

8.3 Strategies for the Last Touch

The last touch is naturally the most important in a bout and strictly speaking it is the only one that really matters. (If you are 1 – 4 down and you win the next touch to make it 2 – 4, you are in another last touch situation.) The most critical and most mentally challenging situation is when the last touch involves a tie (4 – all, 14 – all, etc.). I can only remember one situation when I lost a critical tied last touch. It was in the Heidenheim 1980 European Cup team semifinal against the Romanians, when

I lost my last bout at 4 – all. My teammates were so surprised that they lost their last three bouts and we lost the match 9 – 7.

Winning the last touch was probably the strongest feature of my game. I mentioned earlier a number of features that are applicable to this situation: pressure, nervousness, unwanted thoughts, and Olympic touch discussions all indicate more predictable fencing. In these situations, all fencers would like to work within their particular AoE and, if their opponent does not give the right hidden prerequisites, they will wait a little and then fence that way regardless. I believe all fencers break sooner or later in this situation and try to perform their AoE, even if they do not get the right hidden prerequisites.

Therefore, in a last-touch situation with the score tied, my game plan was the following: I tried to look aggressive and maintain a short distance but not offer any hidden prerequisites. I never attacked, just pretended to. At the moment that my opponent a) performed his AoE out of context or b) gave me the hidden prerequisites for my own AoE, I was merciless. The key was to never change tactics, even for a second, or perform a chance attack, just wait for my opponent's mistake. I enjoyed this situation tremendously because it was so predictable. Sooner or later my opponent's nerve broke and I won. The few exceptions to this rule have already been discussed in this book (Pusch in Heidenheim 1980, Riboud and Kolczonay in the 1980 Olympics). During the whole procedure, I kept my mental balance through "thinking nothing, not even blackness." I did not allow any thoughts or any emotions at all to enter my brain or soul.

8.4 Tactical Considerations

> *The Second – Tai No Sen*
>
> When the enemy attacks, remain undisturbed but feign weakness. As the enemy reaches you, suddenly move away indicating that you intend to jump aside, then dash in attacking as soon as you see the enemy relax. This is one way.
>
> Or, as the enemy attacks, attack still more strongly, taking advantage of the resulting disorder in his timing to win.
>
> This is the Tai No Sen principle.
>
> – Miyamoto Musashi[1]

The new fencing paradigm contains a number of strategic and tactical considerations, mostly from a general point of view. The detailed implementation has not been discussed and is primarily left to the discretion of the fencer. It may be helpful, though, if I mention some of the questions that I had to ask myself when I designed my personal implementation of the paradigm.

8.4.1 Should you ever take a break from your plan?

This question could result in a paradox. The issue comes from the following observation.

Suppose you fence according to your predetermined tactics, do not give your opponent any of the needed hidden prerequisites for his AoE, try to force the opponent into your own AoE. The tactics appear to work and you either lead or the bout is even. In the middle of this, your opponent seems to open himself up in a way that you feel allows you to hit him easily with an attack that is outside your pre-decided tactics.

What should you do – seize the chance or stick to your plan? No rule will apply in all situations, but let us play out the two dif-

---

[1] From "The Fire Book" in A Book of Five Rings by Miyamoto Musashi. Again, this is good advice from Musashi. Look weak, get the opponent to attack, and then you can win.

ferent scenarios. You make the attack against your predetermined tactics. Suppose that it does not score and you get hit instead. It this situation I would hesitate to do the attack again even if given the opportunity, since it is both outside the predetermined tactics and the first attempt failed. It could be that your opponent is trying to get you to attack into his AoE.

For example, in the final of the Veterans European Team Championship of 2004 we met a French team that contained some of the same fencers whom we had beaten in the 1978 senior World Championship a quarter-century before. In one of the bouts, one of my teammates, using a French handle, managed to get his opponent to attack three times into his AoE so that he led 3 – 0.

At this point, the Frenchman understandably stopped attacking. This was not a problem, since time was on our side. But my teammate noticed that the Frenchman's foot was open to attack and tried for a quick toe-touch, even though it was outside his predetermined tactics. The Frenchman was prepared and scored easily. We shouted to our fencer that he should not try any more foot attacks, but he only saw the open foot and perhaps thought that it would be a shame to lose after leading 3 – 0. Anyway, he tried the foot attack over and over again and after five attempts he lost 3 – 5. (We took the gold medal anyway.)

I have seen this happen over and over again in tense situations. Taking a break from your original tactics is fraught with danger.

Let us now consider what happens if your attack, outside your AoE, is successful and scores. It is naturally better than not scoring, but there are a couple of points to take into consideration. Before the attack, you had a stringent set of tactics that appeared to work. You were getting your opponent into a situation where he had to do something to win, because it was evident that you would never make any obvious mistakes. Your successful attack might get your opponent thinking as follows: "He made an attack that scored. Interesting. Maybe I can get him to do more attacks. Maybe I can get him into my own AoE."

Another interesting piece of information is that *I regularly gave away touches*. After I won the World Championship, other fencers treated me with respect. When I met much lower ranked fencer, they were sometimes so afraid of me that they did nothing.

As indicated elsewhere in this book, I was not particularly good at handling fencers who did not offer their blades and did not move forward at all. They were probably thinking something like: "He is so good, he is the World Champion, so I will try to make the bout as long as possible and lose as narrowly as I can." In this situation I would make sure that they scored one or two touches with an attack on my sixth side just to make them think instead: "He is not that good. If I do A, he will do B and I will do C and score." If I could get my opponent to think in terms of hitting instead of avoid being hit, the bout was more than half won.

In summary, *I myself never took a break (did not deviate) from my own predetermined tactics* for a given bout, and so I did not take advantage of any opportunities that came my way if they were outside my pre-determined tactics. (My tactics in the Olympic final were outside my normal AoE, but I had nevertheless planned them carefully.)

I readily acknowledge that others may take a different but equally valid position on this issue.

8.4.2 *Deciding on tactics for a bout*

We also need to consider *when and how the tactics for a particular bout should be decided.* I always predetermined my tactics before I went on the piste, sometimes many months in advance. I had an excellent memory of the last bout against an opponent.

The first question was, had I won or lost? If I lost, then I was sure that my opponent would fence the same way again, so I only needed to adjust my tactics to beat him. If I won, however, I had to ask myself, how might my opponent change his game? Then I had to consider the tactical intelligence of my opponent and his coach. Where would they go? Sometimes I had to prepare myself for more than one alternative.

Again: suppose you are leading in a bout. Then you need to consider whether your opponent might alter his game. The risk is that he might start to push and be aggressive. If you give ground and retreat and let him decide the distance, which may be normal or long (assuming that your preferred distance is short), then the fencing becomes more unpredictable, as discussed at length earlier in this book. Your opponent might start performing unpredictable attacks from a distance before you have a chance to do anything. This is not your preferred situation: At the end of the day, you would like to win all bouts in a predictable way.

The way I handled these very common situations was based on the following observations. Short distance combined with staying well out of my opponent's AoE (not give him any of the hidden prerequisites) limited his options. Decreasing the tempo, by which I mean the time between consecutive bounces, gives an opponent more time and thus more opportunity to perform unpredictable actions. Increasing the tempo (small very rapid bounces) naturally decreases the opportunities for an opponent.

Therefore, when an opponent started getting desperate and I could sense unpredictable attacks coming, I responded in the following ways:

1. I kept the distance short,
2. I stayed far away from his AoE,
3. I increased the tempo of my bouncing to retake the initiative and look dangerous but without leaving myself open, thus forcing my opponent to make his attack from a defensive position,
4. I made a counterattack at the first sign that my opponent was going to attack,
5. I normally forced corps-à-corps to exclude any possibility of my opponent scoring with a parry-riposte should my counterattack not score.

(Because my opponent had started the attack, the referee normally judged him to be the cause of the violent body-to-body contact. Since I was much shorter than most opponents, referees often asked me if I was hurt.

I practiced these rather violent moves for several years with my coach Kaj Czarnecki, who was large and had steel plates under his heavy outfit. I knew exactly how to infight without getting hurt.)

The net result was that the chance of getting predictable doubles increased. Note that my strategy is the opposite of what most fencers do when they lead in a bout: they tend to become more passive and to maintain a longer fencing distance.

Another way of planning the bout is *to identify two different valid tactics against your opponent.* I normally started with the tactic that I regarded as second best. If the score was even or I was losing, I changed to the best tactic in the middle of the game. The advantage was that most opponents expected me to start with my best tactic and they had to adjust their game unexpectedly. If I was leading, I waited to change until my opponent got desperate.

8.4.3 What if your best tactics aren't working?

Finally, we need to consider *what to do if you start with your best tactic but your opponent manages to get an early lead.* Here it is much more difficult to give any advice. My most common reaction would be more of the same and then go into unpredictable opportunistic mode. I would shorten the distance even further with the objective of getting my opponent into my AoE. I might even do attacks that are truly opportunistic when openings appear and sometimes even in my own tempo.

8.5 Peaking for a Crucial Competition

It is of paramount importance to control the times when you peak during the season. You need to perform at your best at the time that is most important. I controlled my peak performance using a one-month procedure. This was my preferred system. All top fencers have their own procedures, but it might be of some general interest, since I managed to win four of the five competitions on my priority list. The program is very demanding and is difficult or impossible to combine with work or studies. It also requires a high level of previous preparation. I would start one month before the competition where I wanted to perform at my best.

8.5.1 Two weeks of exhaustion

The first two weeks would be spent training very hard – harder than at any time in my life up to that point. It would be a nightmare experience: fencing many bouts against good opponents, running cross-country, footwork exercises with the aim of increasing my speed (pushing the outer side of the envelope), and exhausting me as a fencer. The objective was that at the end of the two weeks I would be in such lousy shape that I would lose to fencers I had never lost to before.

I would train four times a day for 2 – 2.5 hours each session. I would meditate and sleep before each training session. To fit all this into a daily training schedule, I had to wake around 6 am. Then the day was divided into eating, meditation, sleeping and training continuously until 10 p.m., 5 days a week. The main focus of these two nightmare weeks was intensity and maximum workload.

8.5.2 A week of speed

During the third week, the intensity of training would be reduced. The number of sessions dropped to three per day and the duration of each to 1.5 – 2 hours. I would fence in the mornings and evenings and do something else (volleyball, less intensive running) in the afternoons. All my free time was spent in meditation, sleep and rest. The focus of this week was to improve the quality of my performance and reduce my exhaustion. This was the week for maximum speed training (footwork). Every footwork movement had to be as fast as possible. During this week I would start to beat the fencers that I lost to in the previous weeks.

8.5.3 A week of meditation

The last week before the event would be spent doing minimal training, like 30 minutes a day. Only a few dexterity exercises were performed during these sessions. The main focus was on meditation, which I performed three times a day for 60 minutes per session. Each day of this week I would feel stronger, unbeatable and ready for the competition.

9.

Consequences of the New Paradigm

9.1 Must We Change the Way Fencing Is Taught?

Not at first!

The new paradigm is a logical continuation of classical fencing, and this book is written for experienced fencers. It describes advanced fencing strategies and tactics and assumes that the reader has fenced for a number of years and has mastered the most common actions of classical fencing. It is impossible to understand advanced strategic discussions without a basic understanding of fencing, and the first five years of fencing education should therefore not be changed. The objective of these first years should be to give the fencer as wide a repertoire of classical movements as possible. Competition is a part of the training.

9.1.1 Begin with a wide repertoire

After five years or so, it is time to select the AoE from the fencer's repertoire. If the repertoire is wide, the fencer has more choice in selecting his AoE. The fencing I have seen in many clubs has shown me that many youngsters are not encouraged to obtain a wide repertoire. On the contrary, clubs seem to teach youngsters "something" and then let them compete, with the idea, perhaps, that they will widen their repertoire later in their careers. But since the modern concept of competitive epee fencing includes focusing early on a fencer's AoE, many youngsters are taught a narrow repertoire that gets even narrower over the years. This tends to make fencing less fun – and less successful in the long run.

From the perspective of this book (not simply the classical perspective), fencers need a wide repertoire for two reasons:

a) To have numerous choices from which to select their AoE,

b) To have a broad palette from which to select improvised and unorthodox moves that could help win bouts.

It is therefore counterproductive to teach youngsters a limited repertoire and even more counterproductive to let them compete with it.

Fencing is perhaps unique among sports in that very successful juniors rarely become successful seniors. In epee, only four Junior World Champions have ever succeeded in also winning the Senior World Championship or Olympic title in the more than 50 years since junior competition began in 1956. The only exceptions to this rule are Khabarov of Russia (both senior and Junior World Champion in 1959), Losert of Austria (both Senior and Junior World Champion in 1963), Kolobkov of Russia (Junior World Champion in 1987 and 1988, Senior World Champion in 1993, 1994, 2002 and 2005, and Olympic champion in 2000) and Jeannet of France (Junior World Champion in 2000 and Senior World Champion in 2003). Why should this be?

If a youngster has early success in competition with a limited repertoire, the repertoire may become permanently limited. When a fencer tries new things, these will at least initially be unsuccessful and if that fencer has a ranking to protect he will be less inclined to experiment. I have seen over and over again that talented fencers become successful early on and then stagnate in their development. Fencing is so complex (more than other sports) that it takes 10 years or so to fully educate a fencer.

Since later in their career, fencers will need to limit their repertoire, they must broaden it early in their career.

Having said this, the skills needed by advanced fencers with high aspirations are different from those required in the early years. Their training should therefore be altered to take these new demands into account. The skills needed for the new paradigm include development of the AoE, bouncing, ability to change direction of motion (from backwards to forwards and vice versa) and the speed of the fencer's arm extension. All of these skills need to be trained separately.

The development of the AoE is critical and, I believe, more important than improving the weaknesses of advanced fencers who possess a wide repertoire. In other words, it is more important to make the good better than to make the bad less bad. In competition, you simply do not use the weak parts of your game. For these fencers, some 70% or more of lessons should be devoted to deepening and expanding the AoE.

Traditionally, fencing involves footwork exercises. In most clubs footwork is still performed as standard exercises, where fencers take up a non-bouncing guard position, even though they may fence bouts from a bouncing position. Footwork exercises become even more important with the new paradigm and should mimic the way bouts are fenced. I believe that most footwork should be performed from a bouncing (competition-style) guard. This has three objectives:

a) to increase speed,

b) to increase the ability to change direction,

c) to increase the ability to move forwards and backwards by bouncing.

Most of this book is written for advanced fencers. However, I believe that bout-like footwork combinations with the objective of increasing speed can and should be initiated for motivated intermediate fencers after only 2 years experience or so, as a complement to standard footwork. Care should be taken, however, that the fencers do not injure themselves.

9.1.2 Emphasize speed in footwork

I believe footwork should be performed in extremely intensive sets of 20 – 60 seconds, during which the instructor urges pupils to continuously increase their speed. They should be allowed 1 – 2 minutes between sets for rest, reflection and concentration on the next session. Not even top trained athletes can perform more than five sets while maintaining quality. (If they can, the instructor can safely assume that they have not performed at their best!)

Each pupil should aim to perform each movement faster that they have ever performed it before. Only especially motivated individuals can perform this type of exhausting footwork. Elasticity and springiness are essential and specific exercises should be designed to improve theses attributes. I have found that intensive use of skipping ropes is a good preparation for the bouncing strategy (double and triple skips only!). I still start all practice sessions with skipping ropes.

9.1.3 Accelerate arm speed

Specific exercises to improve the speed of the weapon arm extension should also be considered. This is probably a new concept in most fencing clubs.

We normally start with extensions of the weapon arm, without a weapon, from a guard position. When the student manages to execute a rapid (snappy) extension, it is time for him to try the same exercise with weapon in hand, both in the air and against a wall target, still from *en garde* position. Since the same rapid extension must be executed from absence of blade or a destructive parrying position, these also need to be trained, both by the fencer alone and in lessons. (It sometimes seems a bit absurd when very competent fencers have to start practicing such simple things as arm extensions, but it may nevertheless be very helpful.) Finally, this rapid arm extension needs to be combined with foot movements in such a manner that the fencer scores at the moment when the weapon arm is totally extended. This can only be practiced in a lesson situation.

A point that might be worth considering is that I do not in principle make a distinction between offensive and defensive movements, as I have already mentioned, and as Björne also discusses in his section. This is only one view and others are certainly possible. I believe the deception that results in scoring is similar in offensive and defensive movements and depends primarily on the movements themselves and not on whether they are offensive or defensive per se. For example, my favorite AoE is a sixth parry – bind riposte in one forward movement, which can be executed in defensive (retreating) or offensive (advancing) mode. My experience is that many (but not all) top fencers use similar movements in both offensive and defensive modes. If the reader agrees with me on this point, it is then reasonable to train the AoE both in offensive and defensive modes. I mostly do that with my students in the same session to emphasize the similarities between the two modes.

9.2 Teaching the New Paradigm

I have been teaching for a number of years and my teaching principles have evolved correspondingly. I have found it especially important to make all teaching into a dialog, and discussion of fencing tactics is an important part of the training. Why are we training and competing in the way that we do and why do we win or lose? I have found the following question especially enlightening for the start of a good discussion at a training session:

Assume that you are at a competition with your kid sister, (or your daughter, your younger teammate – a fencer who doesn't know as much as you do, but who will listen to your advice). She has done a little better than expected and advanced a bit farther in the competition. She is about to fence somebody at least one class better than she. OP's favorite movement is repeated, continuous sixth – second. If OP manages to find the blade, she launches a very rapid and dangerous attack that is very difficult to stop. You situate yourself by the piste to see the match properly and to pay your little sister some respect simply with your presence. But as you help her hook up to the electrical apparatus, she turns directly to you and asks you with terror in her voice: "What do I do?"

You know her well enough that she would lie down crying if you offered meaningless advice like "Fight a little harder" You need to say something concrete and helpful, but you have only 15 seconds. What should you say?

At this point I urge all present to write down their particular advice on a piece of paper. I urge my readers to do the same.

I did this recently with the junior national epee teams of my country during a training camp. The resulting suggestions were plotted in Figure 4A, on the facing page.

Figure 4A
What to Tell Your Kid Sister: First Guesses

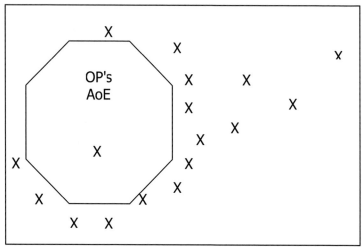

Figure 4A shows typical first advice given by young fencers at a training session about how to handle OP's AoE. Most fencers advised their kid sister to try to attack the better fencer by disengaging away from her attempts to find the blade with sixth – second. This, however, brings sister's fencing very close to the opponent's AoE. One fencer suggested, with unclear rationale, making a straight fleche attack. Two fencers advocated that their kid sister should stay away from the opponent's AoE as much as possible while another two suggested the middle ground.

The discussion was interesting, since, as the diagram shows, most of these young fencers were very ready to send the kid sister right into or very close to the AoE of a stronger opponent. It is obvious, however, that the opponent has carefully chartered the terrain around her own AoE. I selected the AoE to mimic the Soviet fencing from the 60's and the tactics is described in other parts of the book. The discussion coming from this diagram is obvious from other parts of the book and I leave it to the reader to assemble suitable questions for the discussion.

But we can push the point a little bit further by adding the AoE of the kid sister, resulting in Figure 4B (following page).

From this new diagram, and assuming that we advised our sister to stay as far away from her opponent's AoE as possible, we can then ask the following question: Is it possible to get the better

Figure 4B
My Kid Sister Has an AoE?

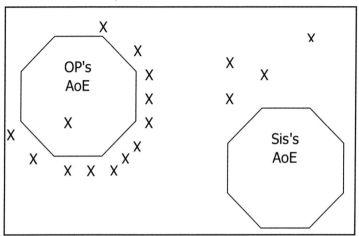

opponent within your sister's AoE? Using the reversed reasoning we must answer probably yes. Since most of us, acting as advisors, were ready to send our kid sister into or close to the opponent's AoE, we must assume that the opponent has advisors that might send the opponent into our sister's AoE. Our sister may not have to do much at all; the opponent might land inside her AoE anyway. This assumes that the kid sister has an AoE, which was not clear from the previous formulation of the problem.

My personal starting point in educating fencers is based on the following reasoning. The fencers need to stay away from the opponent's AoE. They therefore need to be able (at least eventually) to be able to fence with the blade away from the opponent either the "no blade" or "steering" as discussed in chapter 6. In order to fence with a "no blade" or a "steering" strategy, he needs to be able to extend the weapon arm rapidly when the need arises. Otherwise, he risks being hit while he still has the weapon arm bent. Finally, he needs to create an AoE from a "no blade" or "steering" strategy.

These considerations lead to the following educational ladder:

1.   Fast arm extension from guard position where the blade is not pointing towards the opponent,

2. Fast arm extension during foot movements with the objective of scoring at the time of maximal arm extension,

3. Select potential AoE and train it in a non-moving position (immobility),

4. AoE from a defensive position,

5. AoE as an offensive action.

I try to get the student to master one step before entering the next. In practice, however, the steps end up overlapping.

This educational ladder assumes that the student has mastered bouncing. Most experienced fencers have in my experience at least a basic proficiency in bouncing. After the student has mastered all five steps, it is time for advanced tactics where we ask questions like "How can I get an unwilling opponent into my AoE?" and focus on personalizing the training after the individual.

9.3 Can the New Paradigm be Countered?

After I won the World Championship in 1977, there were some early attempts to counter the new paradigm. These included the classical approach, increased or decreased tempo, absence of blade, copying the new paradigm, and combinations thereof. Following the failure to counter the new paradigm, it was adopted worldwide.

The classical approach attempts to turn the predictability of an opponent's AoE against himself. The problem comes when the opponent has thoroughly chartered the various possibilities within his own AoE. One example of the classical approach is to give me my AoE, that is my sixth parry, by feinting into my sixth line and then disengage out of it.

But I have seen this attempt many times before and have trained my move into sixth as a parry – bind – extension in one action, which makes disengaging very difficult. I still love it when people try.

The Germans tried for a short time to bounce even more than I did without copying other aspects of the paradigm. I had researched the bouncing more than they had and this was not successful. It was easy to maneuver my bounces (forward and backward) in such a fashion that we ended up close enough for me to take my favorite sixth parry – bind action. Remember that the Germans at that time stood on guard in a classical manner, with a half-extended weapon arm. I did not have to lunge, just extend – advance.

The Swiss pioneered a strategy of lowering the tempo combined with absence of blade. The rationale was as follows. I wanted to get my opponent to make an advance in order to get him into my AoE with a fixed back foot. My short distance and bouncing strategy made all classical advances very risky. To advance from a short distance would open up my opponent to a counterattack. If he made few advances and presented no blade, that was more of a challenge. However, this was purely a defensive strategy with no means of scoring. It worked well if the Swiss got an early lead, so my aim was to get these defensive fencers to make some sort of attacking movement.

The rational approach was to copy the paradigm. This was first done by the Poles and it surprised me in the 1980 Olympics. The Russians were one of the last to change, but the transition was complete by 1989. As I recounted in the Introduction, Boris Lukomski ruefully told me in Estonia that year," Isn't it terrible – and it's all your fault …"

10.

Afterword

Eric Sollee and his three conjectures had more far-reaching effects than we could have dreamed of.

One of the virtues of fencing is that people can fence all their lives. The oldest active fencer in our club is more than 90 years old. To fence is to have something in common with other fencers regardless of educational background, age, sex, race, income, language, and other factors that tend to separate people from each other. It is a great way of communicating between generations. I have fenced Knut Enell, who fenced in the 1912 Olympics – and he was not young even then.

One day Hans Drakenberg (1935 World Champion) showed up in the fencing room. He was old, and I was in my prime. I immediately attacked him, and he sharply reprimanded me: I had not crossed blades. For him, all fencing started with the crossing of the blades. So I fenced him on his terms, starting from crossed blades, but it proved to be very difficult to score. I could not believe my eyes. He was old, slow, and round. Yet if I started with crossed blades, I had problems hitting him because his hand was so sensitive and he reacted so beautifully to the feel of the blades. For him, fencing without more or less continuous blade contact was simply not fencing.

Edoardo Mangiarotti is perhaps the most successful fencer of all time. He won no fewer than 39 medals in World Championships and Olympic Games, even though the Second World War interrupted his career. His thoughts on modern fencing:

> "Fencing has changed a lot and, in my opinion, mainly to its detriment. It has become faster, technique has lost its importance and physical abilities

have gained ground. Today's accelerated style of fencing can hardly be followed by TV viewers."[1]

Aldo Nadi spent a substantial part of his autobiography trying to persuade the reader that he was the greatest fencer of all time.[2] It is interesting to address the hypothetical question of how a fencer using the new paradigm would perform against such an opponent. From his autobiography, his book of fencing instruction[3], and the cover of William M. Gaugler's *Dictionary of Universally Used Fencing Terminology*[4], it is clear that Nadi had a standard sixth guard, an arm that was at least half-extended, and that he willingly gave blade contact. It should be very easy to beat him under the new paradigm because he provides all the hidden prerequisites that are needed. On the other hand, Aldo Nadi probably would never have regarded our way of practicing the sport as fencing.

It is the irony of fate that I fully embraced all the virtues and ideals of classical fencing, but was destined to become the one who helped destroy them irreversibly.

[1] *The Flame, Magazine of the World Olympians Association*, Number 12, 2004.
[2] Aldo Nadi , *The Living Sword*. (Sunrise, FL: Laureate Press, 1995).
[3] Aldo Nadi, *On Fencing*. (Bangor, Maine: Laureate Press, [1943] 1996).
[4] Bangor, Maine: Laureate Press, 1997.

Appendix

Scientific Studies of Fencing

Ruggero Ceci and I have compiled and summarized all of the literature that is available within the public domain in the area of predictions of fencing success. This is presented in below in a scientific format to separate scientifically verified data from the rest of the book. This chapter can be read independently and can be omitted by those who are not specifically interested in the science of fencing. The chapter adds to the general discussion in this book only to a minor extent. Some of the data were, however, of key importance for us to finally understand that we were on the right track in our way of thinking.

There is surprisingly little scientific literature available about predicting fencing success in comparison to most other sports. This is surprising not only because of the large amount of non-scientific literature published, but also since fencing is extraordinarily suitable for scientific studies, as all hits and movements can be measured electronically. We hope that this chapter will stimulate others to expand the scientific knowledge in this important area of prediction of fencing success.

"Predicting Fencing Success Using Scientific Assessments,"
By Johan Harmenberg and Ruggero Ceci

Research has been performed during the last 40 years to identify measurable parameters that could predict fencing success. Most of the studies have measured the speed and accuracy of fencing movements and have attempted to relate these parameters to fencing success. Singer (5) used 66 female college fencers and Bauchmoyer and Lafevers (1) enrolled 59 female college fencers. Ketlinski and Pickens (3) studied the top 72 fencers at the NCAA championship. None of the studies could show any correlation between speed or accuracy of fencing motion and success.

Stulrajter compared the reaction time of nine experienced female fencers and ten less experienced male fencers (6). The results indicated that the female fencers might have a shorter reaction time than the male fencers, when measured during concentration distraction. No attempt was made to correlate the measurements with fencing success. Also the effect of directional uncertainty on reaction time and movement time during a lunge has been measured in 15 right-handed undergraduates following 30 hours of fencing instructions (4).

Williams and Walmsley studied three expert New Zealand fencers and compared them with three novice fencers (8,9).

In their first study, they initiated lunges with a light (8). During the action, the fencers may receive another light signal that would alter the target. The results showed that the expert fencers had a shorter reaction time, while the novice fencers, surprisingly, had a shorter movement time. The expert fencers had a somewhat faster overall response time (reaction time + movement time)

In their second study, they compared isolated weapon arm extension, arm extension combined with a step forward and arm extension combined with a lunge again with the choice of target. In this study the three elite fencers showed generally a shorter reaction time and total response time and displayed a higher level of accuracy.

Yiou and Do performed a very interesting study where they compared four international level French fencers with five novice fencers (10). Arm extension and lunge were first studied separately. The results could not separate elite from novice fencers. They were then instructed to initiate an arm extension followed as soon as possible by a lunge. In this situation, the elite fencers reached a higher foil speed than the novice fencers. The elite fencers combined foot speed with arm speed better than the novices, who made little use of foot speed. The authors further showed that the arm speed in elite fencers was about twice as fast as the foot speed during a lunge. It should however be noted that the distance from the tip of the point to the target was only 20 cm. The measured speeds are therefore not representative for the maximally possible point and foot speeds.

The research in the studies cited above measured very simplistic fencing actions, like the movement time and reaction time of a lunge from a non-moving state to the hitting of a target following a light signal. Many of the studies used inexperienced fencers. None of the studies could show correlations between the measured parameters and fencing success within any group. In addition most studies showed the difficulty of finding parameters that could distinctly separate expert fencers from novice fencers.

We therefore initiated studies of more fencing-like situations and used top international fencers as test subjects, including Olympic medalists (2). Three different test situations were created. The first was similar to previous studies. The reaction time and movement time were simply measured from a non-moving position to hitting a target on a wall with a lunge. The movement was initiated with a light. This test could not differentiate between top fencers and beginners and did not correlate with fencing success among the top fencers. This negative result was similar to previous studies.

The second test was similar to the first in that movement was initiated from a non-moving position, but the target was a fencing master and the movement was initiated by the extension of the fencing master's arm. The movement was not a simple lunge but rather a running attack (fleche). This procedure was more fencing-like than the previous. This test situation could not, however, differentiate top fencers from beginners, nor did it correlate with fencing success among the top fencers.

A third test was similar to the second with the exception that the movement (fleche) was initiated from a retreating situation (the fencing master advancing) and the test subject had to bind the fencing master's blade during the fleche. This test was thus the most realistic. It was able to differentiate top fencers from beginners and correlate the reaction time with success within the group of top fencers. We therefore proposed that the ability to initiate a forward motion (in this case a fleche) from a continuous retreating situation might be of importance for fencing success.

As a final note, I cannot resist the temptation to also include a reference from the scientific literature to Eric Sollee's work with blind fencers (7).

References

1. Bauchmoyer S. and V. Lefevers. Relationships between components of speed, accuracy and fencing success. *U.S. Department of Health, Education and Welfare. National Institute of Education*, 1975

2. Harmenberg J., R. Ceci, P. Barvestad, K. Hjerpe, and B. Ekblom. Comparison of different tests of fencing performance. *Int. J. Sports Med.*, 12: 573 – 576, 1991

3. Ketlinski R. and L. Pickens. Characteristics of male fencers in the 28th annual NCAA fencing championships. *Res. Quart.*, 44: 434 – 439, 1973.

4. Sanderson F.H. The effect of directional uncertainty on reaction time and movement time in a fencing task. *J. Sport Sci.*, 1: 105 – 110, 1983

5. Singer R.N. Speed and accuracy of movement as related to fencing success. *Research Quart.*, 39: 1080 – 1083, 1968.

6. Stulrajter V. Situation-specific reaction time measurement in sportsmen (fencers). *Activitas Nervosa Superior*, 29: 170 – 171, 1987.

7. Tehan R. Blindness is no foil to fencing. *J. Rehabil.*, 46(3): 86 – 87, 1980.

8. Williams L. R. T. and A. Walmsley. Response amendments in fencing: Differences between elite and novice subjects. *Perceptual and Motor Skills*, 91:131 – 142, 2000.

9. Williams L. R. T. and A. Walmsley. Response timing and muscular coordination in fencing: A comparison of elite and novice fencers. *J. Sci. Med. Sport*, 3(4): 460 – 475, 2000.

10. Yiou E. and M. C. Do. In fencing, does intensive practice equally improve the speed performance of the hit when it is performed alone and in combination with the lunge? *Inst. Sport Med.* 21: 122 – 126, 2000.

Discussion

There are two major take-home messages from the scientific literature. The first is that it is surprisingly little that, in laboratory conditions, separates fencers from non-fencers with respect to movement time and reaction time and accuracy when executing simple fencing movements without an opponent. The studies cited could not even statistically separate groups of non-fencers from fencers. This was a surprise to most researchers, since it has generally been believed that years of fencing practice has improved movement time and reaction time and the accuracy of, for example, lunge and arm extensions. But this could not be confirmed scientifically. As discussed earlier, too little attention is actually paid to arm extension speed in fencing salles around the world. This is probably a mistake, since arm extension speed is critical for the paradigm that is central to this book. Arm extension speed can easily be trained and progress can easily be followed by electronic means.

One study compared movement time and reaction time in a more realistic fencing situation in which the fencers, while retreating, had to bind an extending arm and perform a fleche. Not surprisingly, the fencers did better than the non-fencers. The surprising and very important result was that this measure also statistically correlated with a parameter of fencing success *within the group of top fencers* that included Olympic medalists. The accumulated results from the ten competitions that constituted the grounds for qualification to the Swedish team for the World Championship that year were used as the measure of fencing success.

This result is directly in line with the paradigm presented in this book. One of the main ways of using the paradigm is to get the opponent moving forward and to get him to present his blade into the first fencer's AoE. The fencer needs to bind the blade and rapidly start moving forward from a retreating situation, thereby fastening the back foot of an opponent who was moving forward. Since the difference between the top fencers is often very small (they beat each other in different ways in different competitions), it was a surprise that this parameter of fencing success did statistically correlate with assessments of movement time and reaction time in this more realistic fencing situation. This suggests that the ability to change direction of movement (from forward to backward and vice versa) is essential to fencing success and we have proposed that it should be trained separately (see Chapters 6 and 9).

1841698

Made in the USA